LAMB
LOVER'S
COOKBOOK

 Recipes that make cooking lamb a fun and delicious adventure!

Cover and book design by Carol J. Elkins

Proceeds from the sale of this cookbook
support the purpose and program of the
Barbados Blackbelly Sheep Association International

Published by the
Barbados Blackbelly Sheep Association International

The Barbados Blackbelly Sheep Association International is a not-for-profit organization dedicated to the preservation and improvement of the Barbados Blackbelly and American Blackbelly sheep breeds by way of public promotion and education of its membership.

The proceeds from the sale of Lamb Lover's Cookbook support the purpose and programs of the Barbados Blackbelly Sheep Association International.

Additional copies of Lamb Lover's Cookbook and other Association products may be obtained online at www.blackbellysheep.org or by contacting the BBSAI at cookbook@blackbellysheep.org.

TABLE OF CONTENTS

ACKNOWLEDGMENTS

The beautiful sheep in the photographs at the beginning of every section in this book are the pride and joy of the following shepherds:

Darryl and Kerry (whose last name and location are unknown) (Accompaniments/Condiments)
James Harper, Prince George, VA (Casseroles)
Mark Fleming, Lamar, MO (Chops and Steaks, Miscellaneous, Shoulder)
Stephan Wildeus, Virginia State University (Ethnic, Ground Lamb, Marinades)
Beth Stamper, Powell Butte, OR (Welcome)
Carol Elkins, Pueblo, CO (Index, Leg/Rack of Lamb)
Mary Swindell, Cobden, IL (Sausage, BBQ/Grilled)
Matt Rales, Potomac, MD (Shanks and Neck)

BBSAI member Lynn Magedson, owner of Good Earth Organic Farm in Celeste, TX, wrote the sections in this Introduction entitled "Cuts of Meat" and "General Tips for Producers." Lynn sells quality cuts of organic lamb from her farm Web site at www.goodearthorganicfarm.com.

Special thanks to BBSAI member Becky Lannon in Hockley, TX, for proofreading this cookbook. Without the countless hours she spent reading and re-reading every recipe, imposing consistency across recipes from hundreds of different sources, this cookbook would have been an unfriendly jumble of information.

Final thanks to longtime BBSAI member and professional writer Carol Elkins who first suggested the idea of a BBSAI cookbook. She acquired and organized the recipes; designed the layout and look of the cookbook; indexed it; created the front and back cover artwork; and managed the entire production. Without her efforts, there would be no BBSAI cookbook.

WELCOME!

CONTENTS

WELCOME!

Lamb lovers have known for centuries that lamb is one of the tastiest, most versatile meats in the world. It is one of the leanest red meats that one can eat, primarily because it does not have a "marbling" of saturated fat throughout its cuts. And it's relatively low in calories—a 3-oz serving of cooked, lean, lamb can have less than 200 calories. It has plenty of protein and is high in B vitamins, niacin, zinc and iron.

Lamb haters don't care about any of this. They just plain don't like the taste of lamb and that's that. It is very hard to convert a lamb hater into a lamb lover.

But that is EXACTLY what this cookbook can do. We believe that the reason most people don't like lamb is because they have never tasted it cooked properly. Overcooked, dry, muttony flavored meat will discourage anyone from trying it a second time. These folks have probably never sampled a recipe from a culture whose diet is primarily lamb and who have learned to add subtle seasonings to enrich the flavor or spice it up in exotic curries. They never had a chance to simply grill a tender, juicy, loin chop or discover how much better a hamburger tastes when made with ground lamb.

Lamb lovers who have already experienced these delights will appreciate the diversity of the recipes in this cookbook. Collected from over a hundred web sites, cookbooks, and personal recipe cards, these recipes illustrate why lamb is so popular all over the world.

We can't pass up this opportunity to put in a shameless plug for lamb from hair sheep—specifically Barbados Blackbelly and American Blackbelly hair sheep. If you like lamb, then you will even like it more if you locate a Blackbelly breeder in your area and purchase home-grown, pasture-fed Blackbelly lamb. Hair sheep do not have wool. Instead, they have a hair coat similar to a deer or a goat. The flavor of "muttony lamb" is caused by the lanolin in their wool. Because hair sheep have no wool, their meat is mild and sweet, much like a quality cut of beef. Hair sheep are much leaner than woolie sheep, too, making all of their cuts perfect for high-protein low-carb diets.

If you don't like lamb (and we're not sure why you're reading this cookbook if that's the case), then do yourself a favor and try it again, but make sure you purchase Blackbelly lamb or lamb from some other hair sheep breed. A good cut of lamb cooked using any of the recipes in this book will guarantee that you'll become a Lamb Lover in no time!

> **There is more to lamb than just Roast Leg of Lamb with Mint Jelly!**
>
> I'd be willing to bet that one of the reasons you purchased this cookbook is because you already knew that and now you want to know "what else?"

BUYING LAMB

The popularity of lamb has increased a lot over the past decade. This is due partly to European and Asian migrants (historically great consumers of lamb) who have introduced their culinary traditions to other cultures along their travels, and partly to a new health consciousness. Lamb is a good source of protein, Vitamin B-12, niacin, zinc, and iron. It appeals to low-carb, low-fat, high-protein diet enthusiasts and is a good substitute for beef.

There are three basic ways to obtain lamb, and the way you choose will often determine the quality of the meat.

Purchase from a retail market	No control over country of origin, breed, or chemical additives; quality of meat very inconsistent; price very high; cuts of meat limited
Purchase from a local rancher	Almost as good as growing your own, providing you can find a local rancher whose lamb has been raised to your dietary preferences; cost sometimes higher than store-bought because the quality is higher; often available as organically grown
Grow your own	Total control over all food and chemicals going into your lamb and ultimately into your own body; price consists of pasture/grain and butchering costs; you choose when and how to butcher; you choose what breed to grow

For the best meat, grow it yourself!

Because this cookbook is produced by the Barbados Blackbelly Sheep Association International (BBSAI), we would be remiss in not taking this opportunity to persuade you to raise your own Barbados Blackbelly and American Blackbelly sheep for your table. These two breeds of sheep are *hair* sheep, meaning that they do not have wool (and thus spare you the labor and cost of shearing). The lanolin in wool is one of the things that contributes to the "muttony" flavor that many people dislike about lamb. Hair sheep have very little lanolin, and their meat is mild and sweet, tender, and very lean.

Barbados Blackbelly and American Blackbelly sheep are very economical to raise because they are disease resistant and parasite tolerant. This means that you not only save money in vet fees and drugs, but you often can raise your sheep totally free of chemicals. Think about how good you will feel knowing that the meat you give your family is the best tasting, healthiest meat available. Lamb is much easier to store in your freezer, too. A lamb yields 30-40 lb of meat, cut and wrapped, which will fit on one shelf in your freezer. (Okay, if you have a really tiny freezer, find a friend to split an order.)

You couldn't possibly find a more beautiful, exotic-looking sheep to grace your backyard. We have included lots of photos of these sheep so that you can see what we mean. Their meat is superior to any other breed of sheep (of course we're going to say that because it's what our customers tell us!), they are relatively easy to raise, they are great weed eaters, and can thrive even in poor pasture. Because they breed out of season and regularly have twins, you will get more lambs more often.

So what else can we do to convince you?

Even if you really don't have room for a sheep in your back yard, there is no reason to deprive yourself of the best lamb available. You can find a breeder near you who would be happy to sell you lamb any time of the year (not just around holidays). Go to the BBSAI's Web site at www.blackbellysheep.org and have a look at the Breeders Directory. (While you're there, look around the site and learn more about these marvelous sheep.) And when you select a breeder, ask for a sample of the lamb meat. Try your sample out using one of the recipes in this book. You will be hooked…we guarantee it!

CUTS OF MEAT

Regardless of whether you grow your own lamb or purchase it from a producer, butcher, or supermarket, you will want to know the basic cuts so that you can purchase the most suitable cut for your intended recipe.

At the butcher or when giving instructions to have your lamb cut and wrapped, knowing the basic cuts will help you select the most efficient way to use the meat. For example if you cook for only yourself or another person and you rarely entertain, you might not want a whole leg of lamb but instead might choose to have the leg cut into individual steaks. If your family prefers lamb burger over a whole roast, or you like being able to grab a pound of burger from the freezer for a quick defrost, then you might want to have more of your meat ground.

Sheep meat can be classified by the age of the animal at slaughter. Lamb refers to the meat of a sheep less than one year of age. Hogget is the meat of a sheep from one year to two years. Mutton is the meat from a sheep more than two years of age. The main difference we have found is tenderness. Mutton is better utilized as ground meat, sausage and/or pressure-cooked. The flavor of mutton is great, it can just get a bit chewy without proper preparation. Yields from a hogget sheep will be better than most lambs.

The weight and age of the sheep is the determining factor for processing. Small lambs may be roasted whole depending on the size of your oven. They are popular for roasting on an outdoor grill or rotisserie. This is the most expensive way to eat lamb. The cost per pound is high due to the low yield. It is mainly a dish for presentation or ease of home processing.

Lambs that are close to a year in age and 85 to 100 pounds can be processed into most of the American supermarket type lamb cuts. Dressed weight can range from 48 to 52 percent of live weight. Packaged weight of the meat is about 8-10 pounds less than the dressed or hanging carcass weight.

Listed on the following pages are some processing options by the cut, using a conventional custom processor. Any cut can be made into ground meat, stew meat or sausage, so I do not list these as options on each individual cut. They have their own section after the cuts.

Neck	Slice it cross-wise for chops. Neck chops are braised, grilled or used in stews. They taste very much like lamb shanks.
Shoulder	Shoulder chops, shoulder roast(s). A good size lamb shoulder usually makes two roasts. This is the highest protein cut of lamb. It has a complex bone structure and does not slice easily for carving at the table. Shoulder chops are usually best at 1 ¼ in. Because of the bone structure, a lot of meat can be lost attempting to use shoulder as ground or stew meat.
Rib cage (rack)	Rib chops and spare ribs use the entire rack (rib cage and breast) with little waste. The rib chops are cut from the top of the rib cage. The bottom portion becomes spare ribs with a nice piece of flank. Par boil the spare ribs and then broil them, basting with BBQ or your favorite sauce. If not boiled first, the ribs tend to be dry and tough. If you cook them overnight in the crock-pot, they are fall-apart tender and lend themselves well to tacos, fajitas, and enchiladas. Rib chops are usually the tenderest chop, even on older sheep. The rib is the standard of measure for the thickness—cutting between the ribs for each chop. You can trim back all the meat from the rib end of the chop and you have a fancy "frenched" rib chop.
Rack of lamb	Rack of lamb is the rib rack left intact and not sliced into individual chops. The problem making a rack is that most processors do not have experience removing the chine bone to allow for cutting at the table. You can do it at home; just crack the rack between the ribs and it will come apart for serving after roasting.
Shanks	Foreshanks are the mid-part of the foreleg, below the shoulder and above the knee. Hind shanks are the lower part of the hind leg, above the hock joint. Foreshanks and hind shanks taste the same, and are used similarly. You may choose to leave the hind shank as part of the leg, especially on smaller carcasses. Shanks can be cut up for stew meat or left whole. Shanks and neck have a rich, meaty taste that is distinctly different from the remainder of the cuts.
Loin	The loin starts where the rack (rib cage) ends. It can be processed into chops. On smaller sheep, ask for an English chop (also called double chops). The loin is left whole and cut crosswise for larger chops. On larger loins, the loin is cut down the center and chops are cut from each side. Loin chops are often called t-bone chops. They are the smallest chop and often not as tender as other chops. A marinade can be used for half an hour prior to cooking and the chops will be tenderer. Loins can be left whole for roasts or used for stew cubes.
Leg	The hind legs can be cut for leg of lamb, leg roasts, leg steaks, or used for stew cubes. A good sized leg is 5 lb whole. Cut in half for two roasts. The leg can be sliced into any thickness of leg steak. Due to the simple bone structure, cutting legs for stew cubes or ground meat results in minimal waste. If your processor smokes bacon and hams, have a leg of lamb smoked. Sometimes called "lamb ham," it is wonderful when smoked and cured. You can smoke legs at home if you have a smoker/cooker.

Ground meat	The carcass of a sheep parts out very efficiently and little trimming is left-over. Large Blackbelly lambs may have only 4 lb of ground meat from the trimmings. If you desire more, have some of your least utilized cuts made into ground meat. Processors can also make lamb burger patties, ready for the skillet or grill. Request that any bones from stripped cuts be packaged for soup bones. They make great chews for dogs.
Sausage	If you can find a local German family that operates a slaughterhouse, you will discover that they make the most wonderful sausage. You will want to try smoked German, Polish, beer bratwurst (lamb brats), summer sausage, and breakfast sausage. To ensure a lean, tasty sausage, ask your butcher to not add any pork fat, fillers, or extenders, unless you simply want a larger amount of sausage. If your processor makes ground meat patties, they may also make sausage patties.
Stew cubes (boneless) or bone-in stew meat	Foreshanks, hind shanks, and neck can be cut for bone-in stew meat. With bone-in meats, it is best to have 2 lb per package. Stew cubes or kabobs can be made from the legs and loin. The shoulder can also be used, but more meat will be left on the bones. Boneless meat can be packaged 1 lb per pack. Just as with ground meat, request the bones packaged for soup or for your favorite canine.
Organs	Lamb liver is sweeter than cow liver. If you enjoy liver, lamb liver will be your favorite. If you are not into using the heart, kidneys, and/or testicles, consider using them to provide a highly nutritious treat for you dog or cat.
Skins	Sheep hides can be tanned and used for many things. A local deer processor or taxidermist can usually tan hides. Mail order processors also exist and can offer more options for sheep hides. Contact them and they can inform you how to prepare the hide prior to delivery.

GENERAL TIPS FOR PRODUCERS

Blackbelly meat is lean and prone to over-drying when cooked using high heat and/or open flame. Wrap chops in foil, season, and place under the broiler or on the grill. Remember to use a slightly lower heat than when cooking beef or lamb from a wool sheep. Most lamb should not be cooked at more than 325 °F. Lean lamb may benefit from being cooked at 275 °F or 300 °F.

When using recipes meant for meat from wool sheep, we recommend you ignore most seasoning recommendations. Blackbelly meat does not require seasoning like mint, cinnamon, or cloves to disguise the flavor. Such seasonings might be appropriate for wool sheep meat, but unless you happen to like the seasoning, don't consider it for hair sheep meat. Salt and pepper do nicely. In fact, we urge you to try your meat this way first, then decide on seasonings.

When you select a lamb for processing, be sure to check for dates of recent medications. If you use wormers, vaccines, or antibiotics on your flock, read the drug's label to determine the needed withdrawal time. Never process (or sell for slaughter) a recently medicated sheep, a sick sheep, or a bred female.

Ram lambs destined for butcher may be intact or castrated. There is no objectionable taste to the meat. However, meat from a wether will be tenderer than from a ram. The influence of testosterone makes for leaner meat and meat that is just a bit chewier. Meat from a yearling ram lamb is not necessarily tough, but compared to a yearling wether, there is a difference. When selling meat for others to consume, this will help you decide how to manage your male butcher lambs.

Marketing meat from your flock is easy once folks get a taste of this great meat. When you sell a whole butcher lamb to new customers, always discuss the cuts with them. Individual customers soon develop their own favorite ways to use the meat. A satisfied meat customer will return to your farm repeatedly, resulting in additional sales without the costs of advertising.

ACCOMPANIMENTS/ CONDIMENTS

CONTENTS

MINT BUTTER 1

3 Tbsp softened butter
2 cloves garlic; peeled and mashed
2 Tbsp mint leaves; finely chopped
freshly ground black pepper; to taste

Directions:

Mix all ingredients in a bowl until blended. Place a dollop on freshly grilled chops before serving

Note: This is lovely on grilled lamb.

MINT BUTTER 2

6 Tbsp mint; finely chopped
1 ¼ cups boiling water
¼ cup white wine vinegar
3 cups sugar
3 drops green food coloring; (optional)
½ of a 5 ½ fl oz bottle of liquid pectin

Directions:

1. Put mint in a saucepan and pour boiling water over top of the herbs. Allow mint to steep for 15 minutes.
2. Remove one cup of the liquid and place in another saucepan.
3. Add vinegar and sugar and bring to a boil.
4. Add food coloring and pectin, stirring constantly.
5. Remove saucepan from heat. Skim mixture and quickly pour into hot, sterilized jars before mixture sets up. Seal and store.

 FETA AND GARLIC SAUCE

3 roasted red peppers; peeled and chopped
½ cup almonds; toasted
8 large garlic cloves; minced
1 tsp red pepper flakes
¼ cup Balsamic vinegar
½ cup olive oil
⅓ lb crumbled feta cheese
salt and pepper

Note: Good served as vegetable dip, over baked potatoes, or a sauce for grilled meats.

Yield: 1 serving

MINT SAUCE

1 cup cider vinegar
¼ cup sugar
½ cup mint leaves; finely chopped

Directions:

1. Put all ingredients into a saucepan and bring to a boil.
2. Remove saucepan from heat and cool before serving.

CHOPS
AND STEAKS

CONTENTS

GRILLED LAMB CHOPS WITH ZUCCHINI AND CORN

2 shoulder lamb chops; ¾ in. to 1 in. thick, blade chops preferred
¼ cup bottled salad dressing; Italian or ranch preferred
2 tsp fresh mint or parsley; chopped
½ medium onion; diced or sliced thin
2 cloves garlic; diced or sliced thin
1 Tbsp butter; plus 1 ½ tsp
1 medium ear corn; shucked, kernels cut away from the cob
1 medium zucchini or yellow squash; cut into large bite-sized chunks
¼ cup white wine or dry vermouth
1 tsp lemon juice
2 Tbsp fresh parsley; chopped
1 Tbsp fresh tarragon; chopped, or 1 tsp dried
1 tsp fresh or dried thyme; chopped
½ tsp salt
Freshly ground pepper
¼ cup sour cream

Directions:

1. Place lamb chops in a single layer in a food storage container. Spread dressing and mint over chops to coat well; cover. Refrigerate. The lamb may be marinated for several hours or 30 minutes before cooking.
2. Heat onion and garlic in butter in a large skillet; cook 2 minutes. Stir in corn and zucchini. Stir in wine, lemon juice, 1 Tbsp of the parsley, tarragon, and thyme. Partially cover pan; simmer until zucchini is cooked through but still firm, 7 to 10 minutes. Season with salt and pepper; add sour cream. Cook over low heat until liquid is reduced by half, about 2 minutes.
3. Remove chops from refrigerator. Prepare grill for medium-high heat. Wipe any excess marinade off chops; season with salt and pepper. Grill chops 6 minutes; turn. Cook to medium-rare, about 4 minutes. Remove chops from heat; let rest 3 minutes. Divide vegetables between two plates; top with chops. Sprinkle with remaining 1 Tbsp parsley.

Yield: 2 servings

GRILLED LAMB CHOPS WITH FRESH OREGANO AND LEMON

8 lamb chops
½ cup olive oil
1 large handful fresh oregano; chopped
½ tsp sea salt
½ tsp red pepper flakes
1 lemon; sliced

Directions:

1. Combine the oil, oregano, salt and pepper flakes. Pour it over the lamb, turn to coat it well, then add the lemon.
2. Marinate at room temperature for 1 hr. or cover and refrigerate for several hours. Bring it to room temperature before grilling.
3. Preheat a gas grill to hot or build a wood fire. Grill 4 in. or so from the heat, allowing 3 to 5 minutes per side, depending on the thickness.

Yield: 4 servings

STICKY DIPPY LAMB CHOPS

8 lamb loin chops
1 Tbsp oil
5 Tbsp tomato ketchup
3 Tbsp runny honey
2 Tbsp dark soy sauce
2 cloves garlic; peeled and crushed
1 tsp mild chili powder (optional)
1 pot sour cream and chive dip

Directions:

1. Heat the oil in a large frying pan and fry the chops over a medium heat for 4 to 5 minutes on each side until nicely browned.
2. Mix the ketchup, honey, soy sauce, garlic and chili powder (if using) in a bowl. Stir the ketchup mixture into the pan and heat until bubbling.
3. Cook for a further 2 to 3 minutes, turning the chops once or twice, until the sauce is thick, sticky and coats the meat.

Note: Serve with sour cream and chive dip, salad and chips.

Yield: 4 servings

FIESTA LAMB PEPPER STEAK

1 ½ lb center-cut lamb steaks; trimmed of excess fat, and cut into ¼-in. strips
½ cup lime juice; freshly squeezed (about 6 limes)
3 Tbsp cilantro; chopped
1 Tbsp oregano; chopped fresh or 1 tsp dried
2 tsp ground cumin
1 tsp freshly ground black pepper
¼ tsp salt; to taste
4 garlic cloves; chopped
2 tsp olive oil
2 cups sliced onions
1 cup yellow bell pepper strips
1 cup red bell pepper strips
3 cups hot-cooked long-grain rice

Directions:

1. Combine the lime juice, cilantro, oregano, cumin, black pepper, salt, and garlic in a large resealable plastic bag.
2. Sear and then marinate in the refrigerator, at least 1 hour up to overnight, turning occasionally.
3. Remove steak(s) from bag, reserving the marinade.
4. Heat oil in a large nonstick skillet over medium-high heat.
5. Add the steak(s).
6. Cook 5 minutes, stirring frequently.
7. Add reserved marinade, onions and bell peppers.
8. Cook 6 minutes or until liquid is almost evaporated.
9. Serve over rice.

Yield: 4 servings

LAMB CHOPS DIJON

12 small loin lamb chops
⅔ cup Dijon mustard
3 Tbsp orange zest; minced
3 Tbsp fresh thyme leaves
4 tsp packed light brown sugar
salt and pepper; to taste

Directions:

1. Preheat grill.
2. Trim excess fat from lamb chops. Mix orange zest and thyme into a paste. Add mustard and brown sugar. Mix together.
3. Brush about half of the mixture onto each side of the chops and place on hot grill for about 2 minutes per side. Turn and brush the other half of the mixture onto the chops. Continue until done.
4. Season with salt and pepper and serve.

TERIYAKI LAMB CHOPS WITH WHITE BEANS

4 lamb rib chops; each about ¾ in. thick
½ cup bottled lite teriyaki marinade; divided
1 clove garlic; pressed
½ cup onion; chopped
1 Tbsp vegetable oil
1 Tbsp brown sugar; packed
1 can (15 oz) white kidney beans; rinsed and drained
2 Tbsp fresh parsley; minced

Directions:

1. Combine ¼ cup lite teriyaki sauce and garlic; pour over lamb chops in large resealable plastic bag. Press air out of bag; close top securely. Turn bag over several times to coat chops; marinate 30 minutes.

2. Meanwhile, sauté onion in hot oil in large skillet over medium heat about 5 minutes, or until translucent. Add remaining ¼ cup lite teriyaki sauce, brown sugar, beans and ¼ cup water; stir to combine. Reduce heat and simmer 2 minutes; stir in parsley. Remove from heat; keep warm.

3. Reserving marinade, remove chops and place on rack of broiler pan. Broil 8 minutes (for medium-rare), or to desired doneness, turning over and brushing with reserved marinade once. Serve beans with chops.

Yield: 3 to 4 servings

SOY-GINGER-AND-ORANGE-MARINATED GRILLED LAMB STEAKS

4 sirloin lamb steaks; each about ¾ in. thick
3 Tbsp soy sauce
1 Tbsp vegetable oil
2 tsp ginger root; grated
1 tsp orange zest; grated
½ tsp garlic; minced

Directions:

1. Combine soy sauce, oil, ginger, orange zest, garlic, and pepper flakes on a large plate. Stir to blend.
2. Add the lamb and turn to coat. Cover and refrigerate for 2 to 4 hours.
3. To grill, place the lamb on the center of a pre-heated grill and grill for about 8 minutes, turning once for medium.

Note: Mutton steaks can be substituted, but marinate for a couple of days and slice it thin across the grain diagonally for best results.

Yield: 4 Servings.

BROILED LAMB CHOPS WITH ARTICHOKES, OLIVES, AND TOMATOES

Enhance lamb chops with this flavorful and elegant vegetable mixture.

6 lamb chops; broiled
2 Tbsp olive oil
1 can (13.75-oz) artichoke heart quarters
2 Tbsp sliced olives
1 cup tomatoes
1 Tbsp Balsamic vinegar

Directions:

1. Heat olive oil in a sauté pan over high heat
2. Add artichokes, olives and tomatoes. Cook while stirring mixture for approximately 5 minutes or until tomatoes have softened and the mixture is piping hot.
3. Stir Balsamic vinegar into vegetable mixture and remove from heat. Spoon sauce over broiled lamb chops and serve with couscous or wheat pilaf.

Note: This sauce is so good that you can eat it without the chops, just the sauce and some wonderful crusty peasant or artisan bread!

Yield: 3 servings

LAMB PROVENCAL

4 lamb chops
1 Tbsp olive oil
2 garlic cloves; sliced
1 Tbsp fresh rosemary; chopped
1 onion; chopped
3 oz mushrooms; sliced
1 lb tomatoes; sliced
1 Tbsp tomato paste
salt and black pepper; to taste

Directions:

1. Heat the oil in a frying pan, add the lamb, and brown on both sides. Remove from the pan and set aside.
2. Stir in the garlic, rosemary, and onion and cook for a minute.
3. Add the mushrooms and cook for a further minute, add the tomatoes, tomato purée, and seasoning and stir well.
4. Return the lamb to the pan, cover and simmer for 12 to 15 minutes. Serve hot.

Yield: 4 servings

SOUTHWESTERN LAMB CHOPS

6 lamb loin chops; 1 in. thick
1 cup orange juice
2 jalapeño peppers; seeded and finely chopped
1 tsp ground cumin
½ tsp salt (optional)
dash pepper
¾ cup sweet onion; halved and sliced
4 tsp cornstarch
¼ cup cold water
1 cup fresh orange sections
2 Tbsp fresh cilantro or parsley; minced

Directions:

1. In a saucepan, combine orange juice, jalapeño, cumin, salt as desired, and pepper. Cook over medium-high heat until mixture begins to simmer. Stir in onion.
2. Combine cornstarch and water until smooth; add to the sauce. Bring to a boil over medium heat; cook and stir for 1 minute or until thickened and bubbly. Remove from heat.
3. Stir in oranges and cilantro; keep warm.
4. Grill the lamp chops, covered, over medium-hot heat for 12 to 14 minutes, turning once or until a meat thermometer reads 140 °F for rare, 160 °F for medium-rare, or 170 °F well-done.
5. Serve with Orange Sauce.

Yield: 4 servings

LAMP CHOPS WITH CARAMELIZED ONIONS AND SWISS CHARD (WEIGHT WATCHERS)

8 (4 oz) lean lamb rib chops; french cut
¼ cup reduced calorie olive oil vinaigrette (such as Ken's Steakhouse)
2 tsp olive oil
2 large Vidalia onions; sliced (about 1 ½ lb)
2 tsp brown sugar
1 Tbsp Balsamic vinegar
3 Tbsp water
2 bunches Swiss chard leaves; torn into large pieces (about 1 ½ lb)
cooking spray

Directions:

1. Trim fat from lamb. Place lamb in a large heavy-duty, resealable plastic bag; pour vinaigrette over chops. Seal bag and marinate in refrigerator 8 hours, turning bag occasionally.
2. Pour oil into a large nonstick skillet; place skillet over medium heat until hot.
3. Add onion, cover, and cook 20 minutes or until golden, stirring often.
4. Add brown sugar and Balsamic vinegar; cook 2 minutes, stirring constantly.
5. Add water, bring to a boil, scraping browned bits.
6. Add Swiss chard; cover, and cook 3 minutes or until just wilted, stirring once. Set aside, cover, and keep warm.
7. Coat grill rack with cooking spray; place grill over medium-hot coals (350 °F to 400 °F). Remove lamb from bag, reserving marinade. Place lamb on rack, grill, uncovered, 3 to 5 minutes on each side or until desired degree of doneness, turning occasionally and basting with reserved marinade.
8. Serve with onion mixture.

Yield: 4 servings

SMOTHERED LAMB CHOPS WITH ORZO

4 shoulder lamb chops; 8 to 9 oz each
salt and freshly ground black pepper; to taste
1 cup orzo or tiny pasta-like acini di pepe
2 ¾ cups chicken stock
2 Tbsp olive oil
2 cloves garlic
1 anchovy fillet
1 medium onion; about 8 oz
24 small pimiento-stuffed olives
2 tsp fresh rosemary or 1 tsp dried rosemary
1 Tbsp small capers; drained

Directions:

1. Put the orzo and 2 ¼ cups stock in a microwave-safe container. Cover and cook in a microwave oven on high power for 11 minutes. Keep covered until ready to serve. (Or bring 2 cups stock to a boil in a covered saucepan. Add the orzo, stir, cover, and return to a boil. Reduce the heat to low and simmer for 10 minutes, or until the stock has been completely absorbed.)
2. Meanwhile, put the oil in a large, heavy skillet over high heat. Season the chops with salt and pepper. Add the chops to the skillet and brown on one side for 2 minutes. While the lamb cooks, peel the garlic. Drop it and the anchovy fillet down the chute of a food processor with the motor running. While the anchovy and garlic purée, peel and quarter the onion. Stop the motor and scrape down the sides of the bowl with a rubber spatula. Add the onion and pulse just until coarsely chopped.
3. Turn the lamb and brown for 2 minutes on the other side while you coarsely chop the olives. Chop the fresh rosemary. (If using dried rosemary, crush the leaves between your fingers.) With a wide spatula, remove the chops to a large platter in one layer. Pour out half the fat from the skillet. Add the garlic, anchovy, and onion and sauté for 2 minutes. Add the olives, rosemary, capers, and salt and pepper to taste. Mix well.
4. Spoon an equal amount of the vegetable mixture on top of each chop. With a wide spatula, slide the chops back into the skillet with the vegetable mixture on top. Add ½ cup the remaining chicken stock (¼ cup will be left over if you're cooking the orzo on the stove). Cover and cook for 2 minutes over high heat. Reduce the heat to medium and cook for 2 more minutes. Serve the chops on individual plates with the cooked orzo on the side and the pan juices drizzled over both.

Yield: 4 servings

GROUND LAMB

CONTENTS

SLOPPY JOES

2 lb ground lean lamb
4 Tbsp butter
1 Tbsp corn oil
1 cup yellow onions; slivered
1 cup sweet pepper; slivered
1 small clove garlic
1 Tbsp sweet basil
1 small pinch cinnamon
1 tsp chili powder
3 (6-oz) cans tomato paste plus 9 cans water
1 can (15-oz) tomatoes; diced
4 Tbsp ketchup or sweet honey barbecue sauce

Directions:

1. Melt butter and oil in skillet. Add meat and brown. Add onions, peppers, and garlic and continue to sauté until ingredients mesh together. Add herbs and spices. Continue to simmer until mixture is cooked thoroughly.
2. While simmering, add ketchup or barbecue sauce, tomato paste with water, and tomatoes. Continue cooking until sauce ingredients are thickened. Transfer to slow cooker and simmer on low for 2 hours.

If more liquid is needed, use a tomato product.

Note: This recipe can also be a base for chili or meat sauce for pasta.

RICE MEDLEY

1 lb ground lamb; browned and drained
1 package (6 oz) curry-seasoned rice; cooked according to package directions
½ cup green pepper; diced
1 cup golden raisins
1 cup chicken broth
¼ cup pimientos
2 Tbsp lemon juice
½ tsp seasoned salt
½ tsp salt
½ tsp pepper

Directions:

1. Mix lightly each ingredient in separate stages, one after another.
2. Cook in an electric skillet on simmer heat for 25 minutes.
3. Place in a casserole dish in a 325 °F oven for 35 minutes.

Note: This can also be used as a stuffing for a lamb crown roast or a dressing accompanying a frozen turkey roast.

LAMB BURGERS WITH ZUCCHINI TZATZIKI

Lamb Burgers
1 lb ground lamb; formed into 8 small patties
4 pita pockets
3 to 4 tomatoes; sliced

Tzatziki
2 medium-sized zucchini; quartered and thinly sliced
1 ½ cups plain yogurt
2 Tbsp fresh mint; chopped
4 cloves garlic; minced
3 Tbsp extra-virgin olive oil
1 ½ Tbsp white or red wine vinegar
salt and freshly ground black pepper; to taste

Directions:

1. *To make the tzatziki*: bring a medium pot of salted water to a boil. Add the zucchini and blanch for 1 minute. Drain, plunge into cold water to stop the cooking, drain again, and pat dry.
2. In a medium-sized bowl, combine all Tzatziki ingredients. Set aside to allow the flavors to develop.
3. Prepare a medium-hot fire in a gas or charcoal grill.
4. Grill the burgers about 4 in. from the heat until cooked through, 3 to 5 minutes per side, turning once.
5. To serve, cut the pitas in half and place a lamb patty in each. At the table, pass the Tzatziki and tomatoes; the diners can add them to the pitas as desired.

Yield: 4 servings

SPICY LAMB AND BACON MEATBALLS

1 lb ground lamb
1 medium white onion; peeled and finely chopped
5 to 6 rashers smoked streaky bacon; rind removed, finely chopped
¼ cup vegetable oil
8 sage leaves; shredded
1 tsp Tabasco sauce; (or similar hot sauce)
4 oz fresh breadcrumbs
¼ cup extra-virgin olive oil
10 medium sized tomatoes; cut into ½-in. chunks
3 branches of basil; leaves removed but use both leaves and stem
1 tsp sugar
1 tsp salt

Directions:

1. Heat up a deep frying pan or saucepan, that has a tight fitting lid, and pour in half the vegetable oil. Add the bacon and onion and sauté for 4 to 5 minutes to color the onion. Add the sage, Tabasco sauce and some salt and pepper and cook for a further minute.
2. Tip the mixture into a bowl and allow to cool, then mix in the mince. Divide the lamb mixture into 12 balls and roll them in the breadcrumbs.
3. Wipe the frying pan clean, then place it back on the heat and add the remaining vegetable oil. Fry the meatballs to color them evenly all over then remove them from the pan.
4. Keep the pan on the heat and add the olive oil. When it is hot, tip in the tomatoes and stir for a minute. Stir in the basil stem and leaves, sugar and salt. Return the meatballs to the pan and simmer with the lid on for approximately 12 minutes or until the meatballs are cooked, turning them over half way through.
5. To serve, adjust the sauce for seasoning and remove the basil stems, then serve the meatballs and their sauce with either plain boiled rice or mashed potato.

Note: Searing the outer surface of meat develops flavour and color through caramelization, producing tastier meat.

CABBAGE, LAMB, AND PORK TERRINE

⅔ lb ground lamb
⅔ lb ground pork
4 shallots; finely chopped
⅔ cup white mushrooms; chopped
2 Tbsp butter
2 bay leaves
2 eggs
½ lb spinach; steamed and strained
¼ cup cream; 35%
¼ cup Parmesan cheese; grated
2 garlic cloves; chopped
10 sweet pickles
salt and pepper; to taste
thyme; to taste
12 large Savoy cabbage leaves; blanched and drain

Directions:

1. Preheat oven to 350 °F (180 °C)
2. In skillet, sauté lamb, pork, shallots, and mushrooms in butter. Add bay leaves. Cook until meat is done. Drain off fat and remove bay leaves.
3. Set aside.
4. In food processor, purée remaining ingredients except cabbage leaves. Season with salt, pepper and thyme. Pour in a large bowl and stir in meat mixture.
5. Line buttered bottom and sides of terrine dish, or loaf pan, with overlapping cabbage leaves. Press meat mixture into dish and top with remaining cabbage leaves to seal. Place terrine dish in baking pan and pour water in baking pan to come halfway up side.
6. Bake in oven for 1 hour 20 minutes to 1 hour 30 minutes. Remove from oven and let stand for 15 minutes before slicing. Serve terrine slices over a bed of lettuce with crusty bread or melba toast, hot mustard and choice of condiments.

Yield: 8 to 10 servings

FETA-STUFFED LAMB BURGERS

1 lb ground lamb
¼ cup cilantro; finely minced
3 Tbsp fresh mint leaves; minced
¼ cup red onion; finely minced or coarsely grated
1 tsp Thai red chile sauce
½ tsp ground cumin
½ tsp dried oregano; crumbled
¾ cup feta cheese; crumbled
sautéed peppers and onions; see below

Directions:

1. Combine lamb, cilantro, mint, onion, chile sauce, cumin and oregano in a bowl.
2. Form meat into 8 thin patties, about ⅜ in. thick. Place an equal amount of feta cheese on half of the patties. Cover the stuffing with the remaining patties. Seal the edges by pressing them together with your fingers. Refrigerate until ready to grill.
3. Preheat grill to medium-high. Grill the patties uncovered for about 2½ to 3½ minutes per side for charcoal grills, flipping once, until internal temperature reaches 160 °F. (For gas grills, cook covered for 3½ to 4½ minutes per side).
4. Serve on small hamburger buns with sautéed peppers and onions.
5. *Sautéed peppers and onions*: slice 1 red and 1 green bell pepper lengthwise into ¼ -in. strips. Halve a white onion from root to tip and slice into ¼-in. half-moons. Sauté peppers and onions in 1 Tbsp of olive oil over medium-high heat until softened. May be prepared ahead of time, refrigerated, then reheated in a foil packet on the grill.

Yield: 4 servings

CABBAGE HALVES STUFFED WITH LAMB

2 cups pre-cooked lamb; cut into small bite size pieces (or 1 lb ground lamb seasoned and browned)
1 cup uncooked basmati rice
2 cups water or vegetable broth, plus more for steaming
1 Tbsp curry powder
1 Tbsp salt
1 large head green cabbage
1 cup frozen corn kernels; thawed
1 large tomato; chopped
1 ½ cups shredded cheddar or Monterey jack cheese
1 ½ Tbsp parsley; chopped

Directions:

1. Preheat the oven to 375 °F.
2. Place the rice in a 2 ½ quart saucepan with the 2 cups water or vegetable broth, curry powder, and salt. Bring to a boil.
3. Cover the pot tightly, reduce heat, and simmer 25 minutes until the rice is tender, golden in color, and all the liquid is absorbed.
4. Meanwhile, cut the cabbage in half vertically, leaving the core intact. Remove enough inner leaves, including part of the core, to make a large well in each half. (Leaving the core intact will help hold the cabbage together while cooking.) You can steam the inner leaves along with the cabbage halves and save for another purpose.
5. In a large pot over boiling water, steam the cabbage in a steamer basket 12 to 15 minutes until firm but nicely wilted. Remove from steamer and place on a baking pan.
6. In a large non-reactive bowl, combine the meat, cooked rice, corn, tomatoes, and 1 cup cheese. Mix well.
7. Mound the meat/rice mixture evenly into cabbage halves. Sprinkle with ¼ cup of the cheese.
8. Place on a baking dish and bake for 20 minutes until heated through and the cheese is melted and bubbly.
9. Sprinkle each with parsley. Serve immediately.

Yield: 4 servings

CITRUS-GLAZED LAMB PATTIES

1 lb lean ground lamb
1 large egg
½ cup fine, dry breadcrumbs
2 Tbsp prepared horseradish
½ tsp salt
1 can (8 oz) water chestnuts; drained and diced
⅔ cup orange marmalade
½ cup water
⅓ cup soy sauce
2 Tbsp lemon juice
1 garlic clove; crushed
hot cooked rice; prepared according to type and package directions

Directions:
1. Combine the first 6 ingredients. Shape into four patties.
2. Cook the patties in a large nonstick skillet over medium-high heat until browned. Remove from the skillet.
3. Add the orange marmalade and next four ingredients to the skillet. Bring to a boil over medium heat. Cook, stirring constantly for 6 minutes.
4. Add the patties. Reduce the heat to low, and simmer for about 10 minutes.
5. Serve over rice.

Yield: 4 servings

Orange Glazed Meatballs:
1. Shape the mixture into 1-in. balls. Place on a rack in a broiler pan, and broil 5 ½ in. from the heat for 5 to 8 minutes or until no longer pink.
2. Place in a chafing dish. Bring marmalade and next four ingredients to a boil in a saucepan over medium heat. Cook, stirring constantly for 6 minutes. Pour over the meatballs.

Yield: Yields about 36 to 42 meatballs.

BBQ LAMB SAMMICH

1 lb lean ground lamb
1 medium onion; chopped
1 bottle (12 oz) chili sauce
1 cup ketchup
1 Tbsp sugar
1 Tbsp dry mustard
1 Tbsp prepared mustard
1 Tbsp Worcestershire sauce
1 Tbsp white vinegar
1 tsp celery seeds
8 hamburger buns/kaiser rolls

Directions:

1. Cook the lamb in a large skillet over medium-high heat for 5 to 8 minutes, stirring until the meat crumbles and is no longer pink.
2. Stir in the chili sauce and next 7 ingredients. Cook over medium-high heat, stirring often, about another 8 to 10 minutes. Serve on the buns.

Yield: 8 servings

GARLIC-CRUSTED LAMB BURGERS

These lamb burgers are tasty to bite into, with a fresh roasted garlic flavor, and topped with stylish sun-dried tomatoes and yogurt. They are fast and easy to make outdoors on the grill or in the kitchen broiler.

Grilled Lamb Burgers
1 lb lean ground lamb
½ cup toasted wheat germ
½ cup onions; finely chopped
2 Tbsp of water
1 Tbsp dried oregano leaves
½ tsp fennel seeds; crushed
½ tsp salt; to taste
½ tsp freshly-ground black pepper
⅛ tsp ground allspice
2 tsp minced garlic
6 lettuce leaves
6 whole wheat hamburger buns; split and lightly toasted

Directions:

1. Prepare the charcoal grill or heat the broiler.
2. Combine all the ingredients except the garlic, lettuce, and buns. Mix lightly but thoroughly. Shape mixture into six ½-in.-thick patties. Sprinkle garlic evenly over both sides of patties, pressing gently. Place on grill over medium coals or on rack of broiler pan.
3. Grill or broil 4 to 6 in. from the heat source 3 to 5 minutes per side or until no longer pink (recommend using an instant-read thermometer).
4. Line the bottom half of each hamburger bun with lettuce. Place burger on top and spread top with about 1 Tbsp topping. Close with top half of bun.

Sun-Dried Tomato Topping
⅓ cup dry-packed sun-dried tomatoes
water
½ cup plain low-fat yogurt
2 Tbsp fresh basil; chopped, or 1 ½ tsp dried basil leaves (or combination mint, rosemary, or other herbs)

1. Let tomatoes soak in boiling water 5 to 8 minutes until soft. Drain and chop.
2. In a small nonreactive bowl, combine tomatoes, yogurt and basil (herb mixture). Mix well. Set aside.

Note: Topping can be made one day in advance and refrigerated until ready to use):

Yield: 6 servings

HARRY'S GYRO SANDWICHES

½ lb lean ground lamb
½ lb lean ground beef
1 tsp salt
¼ tsp allspice
1 to 2 small cloves garlic; minced
5 6-in. pocket breads
shredded lettuce
1 medium onion; cut into very thin slices

For the dressing:
1 medium tomato; chopped finely dressing
1 cup plain yogurt
¼ tsp salt
¼ tsp dill weed
1 clove garlic; minced
1 Tbsp lemon juice

Directions:

1. In large bowl, combine meats, salt, allspice, and garlic. Mix well with fork. Shape into five 4-in. patties.
2. In a large skillet, sauté patties over medium heat for 3 to 5 minutes. Reduce heat; turn, and cook until meat is done but don't overcook or meat will harden.
3. In a small bowl, combine all dressing ingredients and mix well.
4. Warm pocket breads. Place shredded lettuce in bottom of pocket. Layer meat patty, onion, and tomato in pocket, then drizzle with dressing.

⊿ BOBOTIE

This easy recipe is a South African dish similar to a quiche pie. It will quickly become a favorite that you make over and over again.

1 lb lean ground lamb
1 ½ cups milk
1 thick bread slice
2 onions; chopped
2 Tbsp butter
2 Tbsp curry powder
1 ½ tsp salt
½ tsp sugar
2 Tbsp lemon juice
2 eggs

Directions:

1. Soak bread in cold milk.
2. Fry ground lamb and onion in butter.
3. Stir in lemon juice, sugar, salt, and curry powder. Stir well and cook gently for 10 minutes. Place this mixture into a mixing bowl.
4. Squeeze out all milk from soaked bread. Add the bread to the ground lamb mixture.
5. Add one beaten egg and beat well with a fork. Pour this into a well-buttered pie dish.
6. Beat the remaining egg and add milk from the soaked bread (about ¾ cup).
7. Season with salt and pepper and pour over the meat mixture. Scatter small dabs of butter on top.
8. Place a pie dish in another pan containing water and bake at 350 °F to 400 °F for 40 minutes until the pie is set and light brown on top.
9. Serve with rice or vegetables. Sprinkle with toppings of your choice, such as diced onion, diced tomato, diced banana, and raisins.

LEG AND
RACK OF LAMB

CONTENTS

SPRING LAMB CROWN ROAST WITH VEGETABLE STUFFING

1 14- to 16-rib lamb crown roast; (approximately 3 lb to 3 ½ lb)*
3 Tbsp butter
1 medium onion; chopped
1 large red bell pepper; cut into thin strips
8 oz mushrooms; coarsely chopped
1 large clove garlic; minced
3 packages (10 oz each) frozen chopped spinach; thawed and drained well
¾ tsp salt
⅛ tsp pepper

Directions:

1. Place lamb crown roast, rib ends down, on rack in shallow roasting pan. Do not add water. Do not cover. Roast in 375 °F oven 20 minutes.
2. Meanwhile, heat butter in large skillet until melted. Add onion; cook 4 to 5 minutes or until onion is transparent, stirring occasionally.
3. Add bell pepper, mushrooms, and garlic; continue cooking 5 minutes, stirring occasionally.
4. Stir in spinach, salt, and pepper.
5. Remove roast from oven. Turn roast so rib ends are up. Insert meat thermometer into thickest part of roast, not touching bone or fat.
6. Fill cavity of roast with spinach stuffing. Return roast to oven; cook 25 to 35 minutes or until meat thermometer registers 140 °F for medium-rare to 155 °F for medium.
7. Cover roast with aluminum foil tent; let stand 10 to 15 minutes. Roast will continue to rise approximately 5 °F in temperature to reach 145 °F for medium-rare to 160 °F for medium.
8. Trim excess fat from roast; carve roast between ribs.

Order lamb crown roast from your retailer in advance.

Yield: 5 to 7 servings

BARBECUED RACK OF LAMB WITH ORANGE CRANBERRY CHUTNEY

Lay the racks on their sides to get as much surface area on the cooking grate as possible. During grilling, the marinade forms an herb crust that underscores the sweetness of the lamb. The tangy chutney offers just enough bite to cut the meat's richness. Beautiful.

For the paste:

2 racks of lamb, 1 to 1 ½ lb each; frenched
2 Tbsp extra-virgin olive oil
2 Tbsp fresh rosemary; finely chopped
1 Tbsp fresh thyme; finely chopped
1 Tbsp shallots; minced
1 Tbsp Balsamic vinegar
1 Tbsp whole-grain mustard
1 tsp garlic; minced
1 tsp kosher salt
1 tsp freshly ground black pepper

Directions:

To make the paste:
1. In a small bowl, mix together the paste ingredients.
2. Spread the paste all over the lamb racks.
3. Cover with plastic wrap and refrigerate for about 8 hours.

For the chutney:

1 cup sun-dried cranberries
½ cup cranberry juice
¼ cup fresh orange juice
2 Tbsp granulated sugar
2 Tbsp cranberry jelly
½ Tbsp Balsamic vinegar
¼ tsp kosher salt
¼ tsp freshly ground black pepper
1 pinch ground cinnamon

Directions:

To make the chutney:
1. In a medium saucepan, combine the chutney ingredients.
2. Bring the mixture to a boil, then reduce heat and simmer, stirring occasionally, until the cranberries are plump and juicy and the chutney has thickened, 10 to 15 minutes.
3. Remove from the heat and allow to cool to room temperature.

Grilling:
1. Loosely cover the bones of the racks of lamb with aluminum foil to keep them from burning.
2. Grill over direct medium heat until the internal temperature reaches 145 °F and the lamb is medium rare, 20 to 30 minutes, turning once halfway through grilling time.
3. Remove from the grill and allow to rest for 5 minutes before cutting into chops. Serve hot with the chutney.

ROAST LEG OF LAMB

1 6-lb leg of lamb (see note)
5 cloves garlic; cut into slivers
1 bunch fresh rosemary
⅓ cup olive oil
salt and freshly ground black pepper; to taste

Directions:

1. Prepare your grill for indirect cooking.
2. Pat the lamb dry. Place one of the forks on the spit. Slide the spit through the lamb alongside the bone. Slide the other fork onto the spit and tighten it. (It may take several tries to thread the rod through the middle of the leg without getting stuck on the bone.)
3. After the lamb has been secured on the spit, make numerous deep slits in the meat all over with a sharp paring knife. Alternately stuff garlic and clusters of rosemary leaves into the slits. Don't worry if they protrude from the meat. Brush some of the oil onto the meat. Season with salt and pepper. Use the remaining olive oil to baste the lamb occasionally as it cooks.
4. Cooking will take about 1 ½ hours. For very rare, look for an internal temperature of 120 °F; rare, 130 °F; medium rare, 140 °F; medium, 150 °F; medium-well, 160 °F; and well done, 170 °F.

Yield: 6 to 8 servings.

Note: Have the butcher cut away any excessive bone at either end of the leg so it does not interfere with the forks that hold the meat to the spit.

GRILLED LAMB, GREEN BEAN AND MUSHROOM SALAD

1 (6-lb) leg of lamb; boned and butterflied, fat and fell trimmed (3 ½ lb to 4 lb meat)
¾ cup Dijon mustard
½ cup fresh lemon juice
2 tsp anchovy paste
1 ⅓ cups olive oil
1 ½ cups fresh basil leaves; packed, chopped
1 cup shallots; chopped
3 lb small red-skinned potatoes; scrubbed and cut into ¾-in. pieces
2 lb fresh green beans; trimmed
1 lb button mushrooms; sliced
spinach or lettuce leaves
fresh basil sprigs for garnish

Directions:

1. In a medium bowl, mix mustard, lemon juice, and anchovy paste. Gradually whisk in olive oil. Add the chopped basil and shallots. Season dressing with salt and pepper to taste.
2. Open lamb into a large baking dish. Pour 1 cup dressing over the lamb, coating both sides. Cover lamb and reserved dressing separately and chill at least 6 hours or overnight. Bring reserved dressing back to room temperature before using on the salad.
3. Cook potatoes in a large pot of salted boiling water until tender, about 12 to 15 minutes. Drain well and transfer to a large bowl. Add all but ½ cup reserved dressing to warm potatoes and toss gently to coat. Cook beans in large pot of fresh salted boiling water until crisp-tender, about 8 minutes.
4. Drain, refresh under cold water, and drain again. Add beans and the raw mushrooms to the salad. Mix in another ½ cup of the reserved dressing and season to taste with salt and pepper. Put salad aside at room temperature. (Salad will hold, covered with plastic wrap, up to 2 hours.)
5. Sprinkle lamb with salt and pepper and grill at medium-high heat on a gas or charcoal grill, brushing with remaining oil from the baking dish. Lamb should take about 12 minutes per side for medium-rare. Remove from grill and let stand at least 15 minutes.
6. Line a large platter with spinach or lettuce leaves. Mount salad in the center. Arrange lamb slices around edges of the platter. Drizzle lamb with remaining reserved dressing. Garnish salad with fresh basil sprigs and serve.

Yield: 10 servings

◿ LAMB KABOBS MARINATED IN YOGURT

1 lb boneless leg of lamb; cut into bite-size chunks
juice of 1 lemon
juice of 2 limes
2 Tbsp yogurt
3 Tbsp olive oil plus extra for basting
2 large garlic cloves
salt and freshly ground pepper; to taste
4 medium new onions; quartered

Directions:

1. Rinse the lamb when you get home from the market and put it in a bowl or resealable plastic bag.
2. Purée the lemon and lime juices with the yogurt, olive oil, garlic, ½ tsp salt, and pepper. Pour the marinade over the lamb, then refrigerate anywhere from 1 hr., if that's all you have, to overnight. Turn the bag occasionally so that the marinade fully covers the lamb.
3. Soak 4 wooden skewers in water while you make a fire, preheat the broiler, or heat a gas grill. Then skewer the meat and onions and brush with olive oil. Grill or broil for about 15 minutes, turning the skewers occasionally so that the meat browns.

Yield: 4 servings

HONEY ORANGE LAMB

1 half leg of lamb; butterflied
¼ cup soy sauce
¾ cup Pinot Noir or burgundy
¼ cup orange juice
2 Tbsp lemon juice
2 Tbsp honey
1 tsp dry mustard
1 cup tomato purée
3 cloves garlic
¼ tsp ground black pepper

Directions:

1. Mix together all of the ingredients except the lamb. Place the lamb in a bowl or pan that will not be corroded by the marinade (a glass 9 × 13 pan works well). Pour the marinade over the lamb. Cover and marinate in the refrigerator for 12 hours, turning occasionally.
2. Start a fire in the grill and get the coals very warm but not flaming. Place lamb on grill 3 to 4 in. from the coals. Cook 20 minutes on each side. After 10 minutes on the second side, start checking for doneness. Contrary to many people's ideas, lamb should not be well done but should still be a little pink when done.
3. Slice thin and serve.

JAMAICAN JERKED LEG OF LAMB

This dish was inspired by the wonderful jerked lamb at the Blue Lagoon Restaurant in Port Antonio, Jamaica. For the best flavor, marinate the meat overnight.

6 ½ lb boneless leg of lamb; trimmed, cut into 3 equal pieces and butterflied for even thickness
2 ½ Tbsp whole allspice berries
2 in. cinnamon stick
2 tsp black peppercorns
2 whole cloves
⅓ cup soy sauce
1 small onion; chopped
4 garlic cloves; chopped
2 large scallions; chopped
2 Tbsp vegetable oil
2 Tbsp dark rum
1 Tbsp thyme leaves
1 tsp salt
1 tsp nutmeg; freshly grated

Directions:

1. In a medium skillet, combine the allspice, cinnamon, peppercorns, and cloves and cook over moderate heat until lightly toasted, about 1 minute.
2. Transfer the spices to a plate and let cool, then grind them to a powder in a spice grinder.
3. In a food processor, combine the soy sauce, onion, garlic, scallions, oil, rum, thyme, salt, nutmeg, and ground spices and process to a paste. In a large shallow dish, coat the lamb with the marinade. Cover and refrigerate overnight.
4. Light a grill or preheat a broiler. Grill the lamb over a moderately high flame or broil for about 10 minutes per side for medium-rare, rotating and turning the meat for even cooking. Transfer the lamb to a cutting board and let stand, loosely covered with foil, for 10 minutes.
5. Carve the lamb across the grain and serve hot.

Yield: 12 servings

ROAST LAMB (CLAY POT)

4 lb leg of lamb
4 cloves garlic
8 sprigs rosemary
salt and pepper; to taste
1 cup red wine
4 Tbsp butter
3 Tbsp all-purpose flour
red currant or mint jelly; to serve

Directions:

1. Make small deep cuts into the meat. Cut each garlic clove in half or quarters lengthwise, then insert the pieces in the slits in the meat.
2. Do the same with the rosemary.
3. Place the joint in the soaked clay pot and season well.
4. Cover the pot and place in the cold oven. Set the oven at 425 °F.
5. Cook for 1 hour.
6. Heat the wine in a small saucepan until just warm, then pour it over the lamb.
7. Cook, covered, for 30 minutes.
8. Pour 2 cups hot water around the lamb and cook, covered, for a further 40 to 50 minutes.
9. Meanwhile, beat the butter and flour to a paste.
10. Transfer the meat to a platter, tent with foil, and set aside.
11. Strain the cooking liquid into a saucepan and bring to simmering point.
12. Gradually add knobs of the butter mixture, whisking all the time.
13. Simmer for 3 minutes, whisking, until thickened. Taste for seasoning.
14. Carve the lamb and serve with seasonal vegetables, the sauce, and red currant or mint jelly.

Yield: 6 servings

GRILLED SHISH KABOB (WEIGHT WATCHERS)

If you use bamboo skewers in place of metal ones, soak them in water for 15 minutes before threading the meat and vegetables onto them; this will help prevent the skewers from burning during cooking. Serve kabobs with rice, couscous or a rice salad.

15 oz boneless lean leg of lamb; cut into 1-in. cubes
1 Tbsp plus 1 tsp olive oil
1 Tbsp fresh lemon juice
4 garlic cloves; crushed
½ tsp freshly ground black pepper
½ tsp dried oregano
pinch cinnamon
2 cups pearl onions
2 cups whole medium mushrooms; woody ends trimmed
1 medium red or yellow bell pepper; cut into 1-in. squares
4 small plum tomatoes
½ tsp salt
1 lemon; cut into wedges

Directions:
1. To prepare marinade, in a gallon-size resealable plastic bag, combine oil, juice, garlic, black pepper, oregano, and cinnamon; add lamb. Seal bag, squeezing out air; turn to coat lamb. Refrigerate 2 hours or overnight, turning bag occasionally.
2. Spray rack in broiler pan with nonstick cooking spray and preheat broiler, or preheat outdoor barbecue grill according to manufacturer's directions.
3. Add onions, mushrooms, bell pepper, and tomatoes to lamb mixture; turn to coat. Drain and discard marinade.
4. Alternating ingredients, onto four long metal skewers, thread an equal amount of lamb and vegetables; grill over hot coals or place onto prepared rack in broiler pan and broil 4 in. from heat, turning as needed, 6 to 8 minutes, until lamb is cooked through and vegetables are lightly browned.
5. Transfer kabobs to each of four plates; sprinkle evenly with salt.
6. Serve with lemon wedges.

Yield: 4 servings

SAUSAGE

CONTENTS

SUMMER SAUSAGE FROM MY GRANNY RUBY

5 lb ground lamb
3 Tbsp meat tenderizer
2 ½ tsp coarse black pepper
2 ½ tsp garlic powder
2 ½ tsp mustard seed
2 ½ tsp liquid smoke
¼ tsp red pepper

Directions:

1. Mix together all ingredients in a large pan.
2. Place mixture in an air tight container; chill.
3. Knead 5 minutes a day for 4 days. On the fourth day, shape mixture into 6 sticks.
4. Place on a broiler pan rack.
5. Bake at 225 °F for 5 to 6 hours. Sticks become red and shiny when done.
6. May be eaten warm or cold. You may wrap sausage in foil or plastic wrap and freeze.

INTERNATIONAL LAMB SAUSAGE (NO SAUSAGE MACHINE NECESSARY)

You won't need any machines to make this sausage. It is easy to make, has no artificial ingredients," and is skinless, too. This is an "easy" home-made version.

1 ½ lb ground lamb
¾ cup onion; finely minced
⅔ cup fresh parsley; minced
½ cup fresh cilantro; minced
½ cup green onions; minced, both the white and green parts
⅓ cup dry white bread crumbs; dried
1 egg; beaten
3 Tbsp fresh mint; minced
2 Tbsp lemon juice; fresh
1 ½ Tbsp Hungarian sweet paprika
1 Tbsp lemon peel; grated
2 large garlic cloves; minced
1 ½ tsp of salt; to taste
1 tsp ground cumin; to taste
¼ tsp cayenne pepper; to taste

Directions:

1. Combine all the ingredients in a large bowl. Mix Well.
2. Cover bowl and refrigerate for 12 hours or overnight.
3. Line a baking sheet with plastic wrap/waxed paper.
4. Using wet hands, shape ¼ cup mixture between palms into 2 ½-in.-long by 1 ¼-in.-wide sausage.
5. Repeat with the remaining mixture.
6. Set on the baking sheet. Cover and chill an hour or more.

Yield: about 18 sausages.

LAMB SAUSAGE EXTRAORDINARE

1 ½ lb lamb shoulder
1 ½ lb beef chuck
1 large onion
4 cloves garlic
1 in. ginger; peeled
¾ cups cilantro
2 Tbsp curry powder
1 ½ tsp salt
1 tsp cayenne pepper
2 eggs
1 cup bread crumbs
1 to 2 lemons
1 to 2 limes

Directions:

1. Grind lamb and beef.
2. Process onion, garlic, and ginger in a food processor until minced. Add cilantro and process to make a paste. Add to meat with curry, salt, cayenne, and eggs. Mix well, adding up to 1 cup bread crumbs if the mixture is too moist. Stuff into hog casings.
3. Serve with warm pita bread with yogurt or tzatziki sauce (see page 23.

Note: These sausages are great when grilled. When cooked, squeeze lemons and limes over the sausages.

EXOTIC LAMB SAUSAGE

Use this sausage recipe to stuff onions, mushrooms, peppers, or in recipes calling for any kind of sausage. It does not require casing.

2 lb lamb shoulder, stew meat, or neck bones; boned
1 cup onions; diced
10 garlic cloves; crushed
2 scallions; chopped
2 cups pomegranate juice
8 Tbsp red wine
4 Tbsp olive oil (fruity rather than virgin)
½ lb pork shoulder; cut in to 1-in. cubes and chilled (optional)
10 oz. beef suet or pork fat-back (see note); cut into ½-in. cubes and chilled
4 tsp whole cumin seeds
½ tsp ground cloves
2 tsp ground cinnamon
2 tsp cayenne pepper
1 ½ tsp nutmeg
4 tsp salt
2 Tbsp cream sherry
4 Tbsp currants; (optional)
4 Tbsp almonds; slivered and toasted

Directions:

1. Trim the lamb of all fat and gristle and cut into 1-in. cubes. Combine in a large bowl with the onions, garlic, scallions, 1 cup of pomegranate juice, 4 Tbsp red wine, and the olive oil. Cover and refrigerate overnight.
2. The next day, remove the lamb, onion, garlic, and scallion from the marinade, discard the liquid, and return to the fridge. Chill the meat grinder parts for about 15 minutes. Working quickly to keep the meat chilled, grind the lamb mix to a medium grind. Grind the beef suet or port fat-back (well-chilled) and optional pork shoulder, and add to the mix.
3. Add the rest of the seasonings and the remaining red wine and sherry. Toss and mix gently. In a small saucepan over medium heat, boil the remaining cup of pomegranate juice, reducing to about 4 Tbsp, and set aside. When cooled, add the juice, optional currants, and the almonds to the meat mixture and mix gently.
4. Fry 1 Tbsp of the sausage mix in a little oil to taste and adjust the seasoning. The sausage will keep in the refrigerator for a few days and should freeze well. When thawing, gently remix any liquids that may seep out.

Note: An alternative is salt pork, diced in ½-in. cubes, boiled for 5 to 10 minutes, drained, and chilled. Cut back on any added pork if you are using salt pork.

Yield: 6 to 7 cups.

LUSTY LAMB CHORIZO

7 lb lean lamb shoulder
3 lb boneless pork shoulder
5 lb unsalted skinless fatback
½ cup kosher salt
2 Tbsp freshly cracked black pepper
1 ½ cups paprika
2 Tbsp cumin powder
2 Tbsp freshly ground coriander seeds
2 Tbsp sugar
3 cups (Spanish) red wine
¼ cup finely chopped garlic
½ cup red pepper; crushed
⅓ cup cayenne
10 jalapeño; minced
3 Tbsp oregano
2 Tbsp chili powder
peanut oil for cooking the sausage

Directions:

1. Cube the lamb, pork, and fat. Combine with all the remaining ingredients. Cover and refrigerate overnight.
2. Coarsely grind through the meat grinder twice. Stuff into casings. Refrigerate.
3. When you are ready to cook the sausage, pre-heat the oven to 325 °F.
4. Cut a section of the sausage and wind it in a circular shape in a heavy skillet.
5. Add a small amount of peanut oil to the pan and put it on the burner. As it gets warm, pierce the casing with a small, thin knife every ½ in. or so. This will help keep the sausage from bursting.
6. After the sausage browns on one side, carefully turn it with tongs to brown the other side. Then put the pan in the oven and bake about 10 minutes. The sausage should be firm to the touch and cooked through. If not, return it to the oven and continue to cook until done. Remove and reserve for whatever you require.

Note: You can also use this as a bulk type sausage, and make patties and fry. It freezes, well, too.

Yield: about 10 lb cooked weight

GOURMET LAMB SAUSAGE

10 lb lamb shoulder
7 lb pork shoulder
14 oz of lamb fat; all the fell (the papery outside) removed
8 lb skinless unsalted fatback
3 Tbsp garlic; finely chopped
6 Tbsp freshly cracked black pepper
3 Tbsp fresh rosemary; chopped
2 Tbsp fresh mint leaves; chopped
6 oz lamb glaze; (optional)
4 cups Pinot Noir or other red wine
3 Tbsp kosher salt
3 Tbsp shallots; chopped
5 Tbsp Dijon mustard
casings as needed to contain the disappearing ingredients
peanut oil for frying

Directions:

1. Cube the lamb, pork, and fat into ½-in. pieces. Combine all the remaining ingredients. Cover and refrigerate overnight.
2. Coarsely grind the meat twice. Stuff into casings. Refrigerate.
3. When you are ready to cook the sausage, preheat the oven to 325 °F. Cut a section of the sausage, and wind it in a circular shape in a heavy skillet.
4. Add a small amount of peanut oil to the pan and put it on the burner. As it gets warm, pierce the casing with a small, thin knife every ½ in. or so. This will help to keep the sausage from bursting.
5. After the sausage browns on one side, carefully turn it with tongs to brown the other side. Put the pan in the oven and bake it about 10 minutes. The sausage should be firm to the touch and cooked through. If not, return to the oven and continue to cook until done. Remove and reserve whatever you require.

Note: This sausage can be frozen if you choose to make it in a big batch like this. If not, cut the recipe in half.

Yield: 8 lb to 10 lb, cooked weight.

SHANKS
AND NECK

CONTENTS

POT-ROASTED LAMB SHANKS WITH ZUCCHINI

6 lamb shanks
2 cloves garlic; slivered
salt and freshly ground black pepper; to taste
3 Tbsp extra-virgin olive oil
2 onions; diced
2 cups tomatoes; seeded, diced, and drained
½ cup dry red wine or water; more as needed
1 bay leaf
3 medium-sized zucchini; quartered and sliced

Directions:

1. With the tip of a sharp knife, insert the garlic slivers into the lamb shanks. Season with salt and pepper.
2. Preheat the oven to 350 °F.
3. In a large Dutch oven, heat the oil over medium-high heat. Add as many lamb shanks as will fit in a single layer, season with the salt and pepper, and brown on all sides, about 12 minutes. Continue until all of the shanks are browned. Transfer the shanks to a plate and keep warm.
4. Drain the excess fat from the Dutch oven, leaving about 1 Tbsp. Add the onions and sauté until soft, about 3 minutes. Add the tomatoes, wine, bay leaf, and salt and pepper to taste.
5. Braise in the oven for about 1 ½ hours, or until the meat is completely tender. (The shanks can be prepared up to this point, then cooled, covered, and refrigerated overnight. Remove the hardened fat from the gravy and reheat in the oven or on top of the stove.)
6. Add the zucchini and mix well. Add more water if needed. Return to the oven for about 30 minutes, until the zucchini is cooked through.
7. Remove the bay leaf. Serve hot.

Yield: 6 servings

LAMB SHANKS BRAISED WITH ONIONS AND ROSEMARY

4 lamb shanks
3 garlic cloves; 1 crushed, 2 slivered
salt and freshly ground pepper; to taste
¼ cup all-purpose flour
3 Tbsp olive oil
16 small onions; about 1 in. across, peeled and left whole
2 Tbsp rosemary; finely chopped
3 thyme sprigs; or ½ tsp dried
1 cup Merlot or Pinot Noir wine
⅓ cup parsley; chopped with 1 large garlic clove

Directions:

1. Rinse the shanks and pat them dry. Rub the crushed garlic over them and insert the slivers into the folds of the meat. Season with salt and pepper, then roll the shanks in the flour, patting it on with your hands so that they're well coated.
2. Heat oil in a Dutch oven. Add the shanks and cook over medium-high heat, browning them all over. Transfer them to a platter and add the onions, rosemary, thyme, and any remaining garlic to the pot. Cook until the onions are browned lightly, about 7 minutes.
3. Return the shanks to the pan, add the wine, and simmer until it has reduced by about half. Pour in 3 cups water, bring to a boil, then lower the heat to a simmer. Cover and cook over low heat until completely tender, with the meat falling off the bone, about 2 hours. Serve with chopped parsley and garlic over all.

Yield: 4 servings

SAVORY LAMB AND LENTILS

2 lb lamb shanks; trimmed of fat
1 Tbsp flour
2 tsp olive oil
2 cups chopped onions
2 garlic cloves; minced
2 cups chicken broth (prefer fat free)
1 can (15 oz) tomatoes; undrained and coarsely chopped
2 large carrots; sliced
½ cup brown lentils
1 medium green bell pepper; seeded and diced
2 bay leaves
2 tsp of dried thyme leaves
¼ tsp ground cinnamon
¼ tsp ground cloves
¼ tsp freshly ground black pepper
½ cup chopped fresh parsley; plus a couple of sprigs for a garnish
salt; to taste
1 ¼ cups uncooked brown rice

Directions:

1. Coat the lamb shanks with flour.
2. Brown in a Dutch pot over medium heat.
3. Stir in the onions and garlic and cook for 5 minutes over medium heat until lightly browned.
4. Stir in the remaining ingredients, except the salt, rice, and ½ cup chopped parsley.
5. Bring to a boil.
6. Cover snugly with aluminum foil.
7. Cover tightly with the lid and simmer for 1 ½ to 2 hours, or until the lamb shanks are tender.
8. Discard the bay leaves.
9. Cook the rice according to directions and keep warm.
10. Remove the lamb shanks.
11. Remove the lean meat and cut into bite-sized pieces.
12. Return the meat to the Dutch pot. Season with salt, to taste.
13. Arrange rice on a serving platter and spoon lamb over it.
14. Garnish with parsley sprigs.

Yield: about 6 to 7 servings

BAKED LAMB SHANKS

4 lamb shanks
1 tsp oregano
1 tsp salt
1 Tbsp extra-virgin olive oil
1 medium onion; chopped
4 garlic cloves
1 cup white wine
1 tsp black pepper

Directions:

1. Rub lamb with garlic. Make a slit in each shank, insert garlic cloves, and then season with salt and pepper.
2. Brown in hot olive oil on all sides, in a Dutch oven. Remove from pot and set aside.
3. Sauté onions with oregano stirring for 5 minutes.
4. Return lamb to pot, pour wine over top, cover, and bake at 350 °F for 2 hours. Serve with rice.

LAMB WITH LEMON AND ALMONDS

8 lamb drumsticks (frenched lamb shanks)
1 Tbsp olive oil
1 onion; finely chopped
3 tsp crushed garlic
1 tsp turmeric
grated zest and juice of 2 lemons
1 cup white wine
1 cup chicken stock
4 fresh or 2 dried bay leaves
2 Tbsp almond flour

Directions:

1. Heat a little of the oil on high in a deep-sided pan. Fry onion, garlic, and turmeric for 1 to 2 minutes. Remove and put aside.
2. Heat a little more oil on high. Brown lamb drumsticks in two batches, removing each batch before adding the next. Remove lamb drumsticks and put aside.
3. Reduce heat and return onion to pan. Stir in remaining ingredients and return lamb drumsticks. Cover and simmer 1 ½ to 2 hours or until tender. Garnish with sliced black olives and chopped parsley.

BRAISED LAMB SHANKS (WEIGHT WATCHERS)

2 lb lean lamb shanks; cut into 4 equal pieces (see note)
2 tsp curry powder
½ tsp salt
½ tsp freshly ground black pepper
½ tsp caraway seeds; crushed
½ tsp ground coriander
¼ tsp cinnamon
¼ tsp ground red pepper
pinch ground allspice
4 medium onions; thinly sliced
1 medium green bell pepper; diced
1 medium red bell pepper; diced
1 large clove garlic; minced
2 cups low-sodium chicken broth
2 Tbsp raisins; chopped
6 dried apricot halves; slivered
1 Tbsp tomato paste (no salt added); dissolved in ½ cup hot water

Directions:

1. Preheat oven to 425 °F. Spray 2-quart casserole with nonstick cooking spray.
2. In small bowl, combine curry powder, salt, black pepper, caraway seeds, coriander, cinnamon, ground red pepper, and allspice; rub 1 Tbsp seasoning mixture into lamb shanks.
3. Place lamb in a single layer into prepared casserole; spray lightly with non-stick spray.
4. Roast lamb 30 minutes, until lightly browned. Remove lamb from casserole; set aside.
5. Reduce oven temperature to 375 °F. In same casserole, combine onions, green and red bell peppers, and garlic.
6. Sprinkle vegetable mixture with remaining seasoning mixture; toss until evenly coated.
7. Roast 10 minutes, until vegetables are softened.
8. Remove from oven; reduce oven temperature to 300 °F.
9. Add broth, raisins, apricots, dissolved tomato paste, and browned lamb to vegetable mixture; spoon some of the vegetables over lamb.
10. Bake, covered, 2 hours, until lamb is cooked through and falling off bone.
11. Divide evenly among 4 plates and serve with couscous or rice pilaf to soak up the spicy sauce.

Note: 2 lb lamb shanks will yield about 12 oz boned cooked lamb.

Yield: 4 servings

RICE-STUFFED LAMB SHANKS

4 short-cut lamb shanks (about 2 ½ lb)
1 Tbsp olive oil
2 slices lemon
3 whole cloves
salt and pepper; to taste
1 cup uncooked rice
celery leaves

Directions:

1. Brown meat on all sides in hot oil in heavy skillet.
2. Cover with boiling water and add lemon, cloves, 1 tsp salt, and ¼ tsp pepper. Cover and simmer 1 ½ hours.
3. Lift out shanks, cool slightly and remove bones.
4. Skim fat from broth and bring broth to boil. Add rice and cook 20 minutes or until tender, adding more water if necessary. Drain rice, reserving broth.
5. Mix rice with a few chopped celery leaves; season.
6. Stuff boned shanks with the mixture, put in shallow baking dish and add 1 cup broth. Bake in 350 °F oven for 15 minutes.

Yield: 4 servings

SOUTHWESTERN LAMB SHANKS

Southwestern Rub:
3 Tbsp chili powder
1 ½ Tbsp ground cumin
¾ tsp ground coriander
1 ½ tsp dried oregano leaves
1 ½ tsp salt
¾ tsp cayenne

Braised Lamb Shanks:
4 (1 ¼ lb) lamb shanks; trimmed of external fat
3 Tbsp vegetable oil
½ 28-oz can tomatoes; crushed
½ cup hot salsa
1 to 2 habañero chiles
4 sprigs cilantro; for garnish

Directions:

To make the rub:
In a small bowl, combine rub ingredients. Stir to blend.

To make lamb:
1. Preheat oven to 350 °F. Place lamb shanks on a large piece of wax paper. Use spice rub to coat all surfaces of shanks.
2. In a nonreactive large Dutch pot over high-heat, heat the oil. Reduce heat to medium. Add shanks and brown, turning occasionally (4 to 5 minutes a side). Add tomatoes, salsa, and chiles. Bring to a boil.
3. Cover pan and place in the oven 1 ¾ hours or until the lamb is very tender. Remove shanks from pan and keep warm.
4. Remove chiles from sauce and discard. Degrease the sauce.
5. Serve shanks with the sauce. Garnish with cilantro, if desired.
6. Serve with soft polenta or yellow hominy if you like.

Yield: 4 servings

SHOULDER

CONTENTS

STUFFED SHOULDER OF LAMB

1 (6-lb) boneless shoulder of lamb
½ cup butter; melted
2 cloves garlic; minced
¼ cup fresh tarragon; finely chopped
½ tsp salt
¼ tsp black pepper
¾ cup flat-leaf parsley; chopped
1 egg; beaten
1 cup bread crumbs

Directions:

1. Prepare the grill for indirect cooking.
2. Stir butter, garlic, seasonings, egg, and bread crumbs together. Spread the meat out flat, fat-side down, on a countertop. You may need to cut a bit into some of the interior creases with a sharp knife to get it to lay completely flat. Spread the stuffing onto the meat.
3. Roll the meat into a tight log and tie it together. With a long piece of string, make a loop at one end of the roast and tighten with a slip-knot. Twist the string into a second loop and slip it onto the roast, an inch or two from the first, and continue looping string down the length of the roast, cinching each loop snugly as you go. Thread the spit through the center of the meat.
4. Place the spit with the meat on the rotisserie. Cook to desired doneness, refreshing coals as needed; it will take about an hour and 45 minutes. For very rare, look for an internal temperature of 120 °F; rare, 130 °F; medium-rare, 140 °F; medium, 150 °F; medium-well, 160 °F; and well done, 170 °F.
5. When done, remove the meat to a cutting board, cover loosely with aluminum foil, and allow to rest 15 minutes before cutting into ½-in. slices.

Yield: 8 servings

LAMB WITH APRICOTS

1 boneless lamb shoulder roast (2 ½ to 3 lb); cubed
1 large onion; chopped
2 Tbsp olive or vegetable oil
1 tsp each ground cumin, cinnamon and coriander
salt and pepper; to taste
½ cup dried apricots; halved
¼ cup orange juice
1 Tbsp ground almonds
½ tsp grated orange peel
1 ¼ cups chicken broth
1 Tbsp sesame seeds; toasted

Directions:

1. In a large skillet, sauté onion in oil until tender. Add the lamb, cumin, cinnamon, coriander, salt, and pepper.
2. Cook and stir for 5 minutes or until meat is browned.
3. Add apricots, orange juice, almonds, and orange peel.
4. Transfer to a 2 ½ quart baking dish. Stir in broth.
5. Cover and bake at 350 °F for 1 ½ hours or until meat is tender. Sprinkle with sesame seeds.

LAMB WITH LENTILS, PEARL ONIONS AND ROSEMARY

12 oz lamb shoulder; well trimmed, cut into ½-in. cubes
1 Tbsp plus 1 tsp olive oil
½ cup onion; chopped
1 garlic clove; finely chopped
½ tsp dried rosemary
½ tsp dried thyme
salt and freshly ground black pepper; to taste
1 can (16 oz) Italian plump tomatoes with juices
1 ½ cups small fried or brown lentils; rinsed and sorted lentil seasonings
1 bay leaf
1 garlic clove
1 celery top
8 oz (about 12) small white onions; peeled
1 cup thawed frozen green peas

Directions:

1. Brown the lamb in 1 Tbsp of the oil in a large nonstick skillet. Add the onion, garlic, rosemary, thyme, salt and pepper; cook, stirring 5 minutes. Add the tomatoes, breaking up with side of spoon. Cover and cook over low heat until meat is tender, about 1 hour.
2. Meanwhile, cook the lentils in plenty of boiling, unsalted water with the bay leaf, garlic, and celery top, until tender, about 20 minutes. Drain. Discard seasonings.
3. In a separate skillet, brown the small white onions in the remaining 1 tsp oil over high heat. Reduce heat, cover and cook the onions until tender, about 5 minutes. Season with salt and pepper.
4. Add the onions, lentils, and peas to the skillet with the cooked lamb. Stir to blend; heat through. Season to taste.

LAMB FRICASSEE WITH LETTUCE

2 ½ lb shoulder lamb; cut up
2 onion; sliced
5 chives; sliced
½ cup butter
2 Tbsp flour
2 heads lettuce, cut as for salad lettuce
4 cups hot water
2 Tbsp salt
½ tsp pepper
½ cup parsley or dill
3 egg yolks
lemon

Directions:

1. Sauté meat and onions in butter. Sprinkle flour over and mix well.
2. Add lettuce, water, salt, pepper, and parsley or dill.
3. Simmer, covered, until meat is tender (about 1 hour). Remove from heat.
4. *For egg and lemon sauce*: beat egg yolks with 2 Tbsp of water. Add lemon juice. Beat in, by spoonfuls, about ½ cup the lamb gravy.
5. Pour egg mixture gradually over meat and gravy, stirring all the time. Serve hot.

Note: This dish is also delicious when prepared with artichokes or endive, instead of lettuce.

◿ LAMB WITH HONEY AND ALMONDS (CLAY POT)

It takes only 10 minutes to assemble this one-dish meal.

3 lb boneless shoulder of lamb; trimmed of fat and cut into large chunks
2 large onions; chopped fine
3 Tbsp honey
1 cup raisins
4 carrots; peeled and cut into 1-in. lengths
¾ cup whole almonds
⅛ tsp saffron; or ½ tsp saffron threads
1 tsp cinnamon
½ tsp ground ginger
3 tsp salt
pinch cayenne pepper
1 can garbanzo beans (large can)
2 cups water
1 tsp arrowroot

Directions:

1. Soak top and bottom of pot in water for 15 minutes.
2. Pour all ingredients, except arrowroot, into large round bowl; mix thoroughly with your hands.
3. Place mixture in presoaked pot. Place covered pot in cold oven. Turn temperature to 450 °F.
4. Cook 90 minutes. Remove pot from oven.
5. Pour off liquid into saucepan, bring it almost to a boil, and thicken with arrowroot mixed with 2 Tbsp of water.
6. Pour sauce over brown rice or bulgur and lamb.

Yield: 6 Servings

SPIT-ROASTED LAMB SHOULDER

1 (3 ½ lb to 4 lb) boneless lamb shoulder roast; rolled, tied
herb rub for lamb (see below)

1. Prepare herb rub for lamb
2. Rub herb mixture over surface of lamb.
3. Cover with plastic wrap or foil; refrigerate 2 to 12 hours.
4. Preheat grill for spit-roasting.
5. Insert spit lengthwise into lamb, making sure meat is balanced; secure with tines.
6. Spit-roast about 2 hours or until a meat thermometer inserted in center of meats registers 130 °F to 135 °F for rare and 150 °F to 155 °F for medium.
7. Add more briquets after about 45 minutes to maintain a constant temperature.
8. Remove cooked lamb to a carving board. Cover with foil and let stand about 10 min.
9. To carve, cut across grain into thin slices; serve on a warm platter.

Herb Rub for Lamb
2 Tbsp fresh rosemary; chopped, or 2 tsp dried rosemary, crumbled
peel of 1 lemon (about 1 ½ tsp); finely grated
2 tsp salt
1 tsp freshly ground black pepper
½ tsp dried leaf of thyme; crumbled
¼ tsp ground allspice
2 large garlic cloves; finely chopped

Directions:

1. In a small bowl combine all ingredients.
2. To use, rub herb mixture over surface of lamb; cover and refrigerate for at least 2 hours or up to 12 hours, then grill.

Yield: makes about ¼ cup or enough dry rub for 3 to 4 lb of lamb (6 to 8 servings)

BBQ/GRILLED

CONTENTS

BARBECUED LAMB RIBS

lamb ribs

For the sauce:
1 cup ketchup
¼ cup vinegar
¼ cup Worcestershire sauce
1 tsp salt
1 tsp black pepper
2 tsp chili powder
¼ tsp cayenne pepper
2 onions; finely chopped
1 ½ cups water

Directions:

1. Split washed ribs into spareribs.
2. Cover with sauce, cover the pan, and bake in a moderate oven (350 °F) for an hour.
3. Uncover and continue to bake for another 30 minutes. Turn several times during last half hour to brown.

SWEET & SPICY LAMB KABOBS WITH MINT & RED ONION RELISH

1 ½ lb lamb fillet or lean leg steaks; cut into 1-in. chunks
4 warmed pita breads; to serve

For the marinade:
2 cloves garlic; crushed
1 tsp fresh thyme; chopped
1 whole red chili; or 1 tsp fresh chopped chili in sunflower oil (i.e. Bart's)
2 tsp paprika
1 Tbsp ground cumin
1 Tbsp ground coriander
2 Tbsp apricot jam
6 dried apricots; (ready-to-eat variety)
1 lemon; juiced
Salt and freshly ground black pepper; to taste

For the Mint & Red Onion Relish:
1 red onion; finely sliced
½ cucumber; peeled, halved lengthways, deseeded, and finely sliced
3 Tbsp mint leaves; freshly chopped
2 Tbsp plain yogurt
Juice of 1 lemon
Salt and freshly ground black pepper; to taste

Directions:

1. Place all the ingredients for the marinade in a food processor or blender and process until smooth.
2. Rub well over the lamb chunks.
3. Cover and leave to marinate in a cool place for 5 to 6 hours or preferably overnight.
4. *To prepare the mint and onion relish*: mix all the ingredients together in a bowl, cover, and chill until required.
5. Thread the lamb between four skewers and cook on a hot barbecue for 4 minutes on each side.
6. Brush with a little olive oil, if required. Leave to rest for 5 minutes.
7. Wrap the pita breads in foil and place around the edge of the barbecue for 2 to 3 minutes just to warm through. (If you prefer them crispy, do not wrap in foil; be careful they do not burn!)
8. Serve the lamb kabobs with the warmed split pita bread and the relish, allowing the hungry guests to stuff the pita pocket with the tangy relish and cubes of lamb.
9. Serve with additional crisp lettuce leaves and tomato slices.

Yield: 4 kabobs

LOW-CARB GRILLED LEMON AND ROSEMARY LAMB

1 lb boneless lamb; cut into 1-in. cubes
5 Tbsp fresh lemon juice
½ cup olive oil
1 Tbsp fresh rosemary; or 1 ½ tsp dried rosemary
1 clove garlic; minced
2 tsp grated lemon zest

Directions:

1. Preheat a gas or charcoal grill or the broiler element.
2. Whisk together the lemon juice, oil, rosemary, garlic, and lemon zest in a nonreactive bowl.
3. Add the lamb and toss gently, making sure each piece is well-coated.
4. Cover and refrigerate 10 to 15 minutes.
5. Thread the lamb onto skewers and grill or place on a broiler pan and broil, turning once, 12 minutes for medium. Serve immediately.

Yield: 2 servings

30-MINUTE LAMB GRILL FOR TWO

4 lamb loin chops (8 oz)
1 Tbsp low-sodium soy sauce
2 tsp sesame oil
1 green onion; chopped
1 garlic clove; minced
2 tsp ginger root; minced
¼ tsp pepper
salt; to taste

Directions:

1. In shallow dish, whisk together soy sauce, oil, onion, garlic, ginger, and pepper. Add lamb, turning to coat; let stand for 10 minutes.
2. Reserving marinade, place lamb on greased grill over medium-high heat; cover and cook, basting with marinade, for 5 to 7 minutes on each side for medium-rare or until desired doneness.
3. Season with salt to taste. Serve with sautéed zucchini slices and sweet potatoes.

Yield: 2 Servings

GREEK GRILLED LAMB SALAD (WEIGHT WATCHERS)

For a speedy lamb salad, cook the meat the day before and use packaged lettuce blends available in the produce section of the supermarket.

8 oz lean boneless loin of lamb
2 Tbsp minced fresh oregano; or 1 tsp dried
1 tsp grated lemon zest
½ cup minus 1 Tbsp fresh lemon juice
2 garlic cloves; minced
1 Tbsp olive oil
1 Tbsp tomato sauce (no salt added)
1 tsp Dijon-style mustard
¼ tsp salt
pinch freshly ground black pepper
8 cups torn assorted tender lettuce leaves
2 medium tomatoes; each cut into eight wedges
1 ½ oz feta cheese; crumbled
6 large greek olives; pitted and finely chopped

Directions:

To prepare marinade:
1. In gallon-size resealable plastic bag, combine oregano, zest, ¼ cup of the juice, and half the garlic; add lamb.
2. Seal bag, squeezing out air; turn to coat lamb. Refrigerate at least 1 hour or over-night, turning bag occasionally.
3. Preheat outdoor barbecue grill according to manufacturer's directions, or preheat broiler and spray rack in broiler pan with nonstick cooking spray.
4. Drain marinade into small saucepan; bring to a boil. Remove from heat.
5. Grill lamb over hot coals or place onto prepared rack in broiler pan and broil 4 in. from heat, turning once and brushing frequently with marinade, 12 minutes, until cooked through.

To prepare dressing:
1. In small jar with tight-fitting lid or small bowl, combine oil, tomato sauce, mustard, the remaining garlic, the salt, pepper, and remaining 3 Tbsp juice; cover and shake well or, with wire whisk, blend until combined.
2. Transfer lamb to cutting board; slice thinly. Divide lettuce among four bowls; top each portion with four tomato wedges, ¼ of the cheese, ¼ of the olives and 2 oz of the cooked lamb, then drizzle each portion with ¼ of the dressing.

Yield: 4 servings

◣ BARBECUED LAMB BREAST

3 lb breast of lamb
1 onion; sliced
2 cloves garlic; minced
¼ cup vinegar
1 Tbsp Worcestershire sauce
1 ½ tsp each salt and chili powder
dash cayenne
¼ tsp pepper
½ cup ketchup
½ cup water

Directions:

1. Preheat oven to 350 °F.
2. Cut lamb in serving pieces, trimming off any excess fat. Brown lamb slowly on all sides in Dutch oven. (Or brown in skillet and transfer to casserole.) Pour off fat.
3. Mix remaining ingredients and pour over meat.
4. Cover and bake in 350 °F oven for 1 ¼ hours. Uncover and bake about 15 minutes longer.

Yield: 4 servings

CASSEROLES

CONTENTS

SIMPLE TURKISH PILAF

3 cups mild lamb stock, beef stock, or chicken stock
2 cups Egyptian rice or baldo or arborio rice
3 Tbsp butter
1 tsp salt (less if stock is salted)

Directions:

1. Wash the rice well. Place in a large bowl, add cold salted water to cover, and let soak for 30 minutes.
2. In a heavy medium pot, melt the butter over medium heat. Drain the rice thoroughly and add to the pot. Stir for 2 to 3 minutes, then stir in the broth; taste for salt and add as wanted. Bring to a boil, then cover, lower the heat to low, and simmer for 20 minutes.
3. Remove from the heat, wrap the lid in a cotton cloth or tea towel, replace the lid and let stand for 20 minutes before serving.

Yield: about 5 cups rice

Festive Turkish Pilaf: For a more festive version of this plain rice, begin by browning 1 onion, finely chopped and ⅓ cup pine nuts in the butter. Stir in ⅓ cup currants, and then add the rice and stir over medium heat for 3 minutes. Add the broth and salt, and then add ½ tsp freshly ground black pepper. Bring to a boil, then lower the heat, cover, and finish cooking as directed above.

CANNELLONI WITH LAMB AND GOAT CHEESE

¾ lb ground lamb
½ tsp cardamom seeds
2 tsp cumin seeds
1 tsp coriander seeds
1 cinnamon stick
3 oz soft, fresh goat cheese
1 Tbsp cilantro; minced
salt and freshly ground black pepper; to taste
1 lb fresh pasta dough; or a commercial one may be substituted
½ cup chicken stock
2 Tbsp extra-virgin olive oil
½ cup freshly grated Parmesan cheese
½ tomato; peeled, seeded, and diced

Directions:

1. Preheat the oven to 450 °F.
2. Put the cardamom, cumin, coriander, and cinnamon in a small skillet and turn the heat to medium. Toast, shaking the skillet occasionally, until the spices are fragrant, just a minute or two.
3. Grind in a spice grinder, or a mortar and pestle.
4. Combine 2 tsp of the spice mix with the lamb, cheese, cilantro, and salt and pepper (to taste).
5. Fill pasta as directed (see below).
6. Put the canneloni in one layer in a baking dish.
7. Drizzle with the stock, then sprinkle with half the olive oil and the cheese.
8. Bake until golden brown on top (about 10 minutes).
9. Drizzle with the pan juices and remaining olive oil and serve.
10. Top with diced tomatoes.

Preparing and filling the pasta dough

1. Bring a large pot of water to a boil and salt it.
2. Cut the dough into rectangles about 4 in. to 6 in. (You should be able to get at least 16 rectangles from a 1-lb batch of pasta.)
3. Cook them, a few at a time, for about 3 to 4 minutes each. They should just be tender.
4. Remove carefully and place in a bowl of cold water, then remove and dry with paper towels.
5. With a short side facing you, make a line of filling on each rectangle of pasta. Roll up, then cook as directed in the recipe.

Note: Take fresh pasta dough, cut it into squares, fill them, and roll them up—these are cannelloni. You can take the same dough (and the same fillings) and make ravioli, tortellini, or any other shape of filled pasta that your heart desires. But, cannelloni are the easiest and fastest to shape.

Yield: 4 servings

SPINACH ENCHILADA CASSEROLE

1 ½ lb ground lamb
1 clove garlic; minced
½ cup chopped onion
salt and pepper; to taste
2 tomatoes; chopped
1 can (8 oz) tomato sauce
1 can (4 oz) diced green chilies
juice ½ lime
1 Tbsp sugar
1 package (10 oz) frozen, chopped spinach; thawed and squeezed dry
10 (6 in.) corn tortillas
½ cup butter; melted
3 cups shredded Monterey jack cheese
1 cup sour cream

Directions:

1. In large skillet, cook ground lamb with garlic, onion, salt, and pepper until lamb is crumbled and not pink.
2. Add tomatoes, tomato sauce, green chilies, lime juice, sugar, and spinach. Mix well. Cover and simmer 10 minutes.
3. Cut tortillas in quarters and dip in melted butter. Cover bottom of greased 9 × 13 in. dish with half the tortilla quarters, overlapping slightly.
4. Spoon half of lamb mixture over tortillas. Sprinkle with half of cheese. Arrange rest of tortilla quarters over cheese, overlapping slightly. Spread with sour cream. Spoon remaining lamb mixture over sour cream and sprinkle with remaining cheese.
5. Bake at 350 °F for 20 minutes.

HAZELNUT LAMB CASSEROLE

3 cups diced cooked lamb
1 can (10 ½ oz) condensed cream of mushroom soup
1 tsp salt
⅛ tsp pepper
¼ tsp paprika
¼ tsp onion powder
1 ½ cup milk
8 oz medium egg noodles; cooked
½ cup chopped hazelnuts
1 Tbsp butter

Directions:

1. In a mixing bowl, stir together undiluted soup and seasonings; gradually stir in milk.
2. Add noodles, hazelnuts and lamb; mix well.
3. Turn into buttered 2-quart casserole. Dot with butter and bake in hot oven 425 °F 20 to 25 minutes or until heated through and lightly browned. Sprinkle with paprika, if desired.

Yield: 6 to 8

GREEK LAMB CASSEROLE WITH PASTA

2 ¼ lb shoulder lamb
½ cup butter or olive oil
1 onion; chopped fine
4 tomatoes
salt and pepper; to taste
1 lb manestra (orzo)
1 cup grated mizithra or kefalotiri cheese

Directions:

1. Cut meat into 5 to 6 serving pieces and put it in a casserole (yiovetsi).
2. Add butter, onion, peeled and diced tomatoes, salt, and pepper.
3. Mix well, cover, and bake in a hot oven for 1 hour or until tender.
4. Add 6 cups boiling water and manestra and stir well.
5. Cover and continue baking for 30 minutes, stirring occasionally.
6. Serve at once with cheese.

LAMB WITH CAULIFLOWER (CLAY POT)

1 ½ lb lean lamb; boneless, cubed
3 Tbsp all-purpose flour
salt and pepper; to taste
2 Tbsp oil
1 onion; halved, sliced
1 cup lamb or chicken stock
1 cup dry white wine or cider
½ tsp ground mace
1 cauliflower; broken into small flowerets
1 Tbsp mint; chopped
2 Tbsp fennel; chopped
½ cup sour cream (optional)
mint sprigs
fennel sprigs; to garnish

Directions:

1. Soak clay pot in water for 15 minutes.
2. Toss the lamb with the flour and plenty of seasoning.
3. Heat the oil in a skillet and brown the meat.
4. Add the onion with any remaining flour.
5. Stir for 2 minutes, then pour in the stock and wine. Add half the mint and fennel, and stir well. Transfer to the soaked clay pot. Add the mace. Cover the pot and place in the cold oven. Set the oven at 425 °F. Cook for 50 minutes.
6. Add the cauliflower to the pot, stirring the flowerets into the meat mixture. Cook, covered, for a further 40 minutes, until the lamb is tender and the cauliflower cooked.
7. Taste for seasoning, then lightly mix in the remaining mint and fennel.
8. Serve topped with sour cream (if used) and garnish with mint or fennel, or both. New potatoes and snow peas are excellent accompaniments.

Yield: 4 servings

POTATO AND LAMB COBBLER

1 ¼ lb boneless lamb (leg or shoulder); cut into ¾-in. pieces
¼ cup all-purpose flour
2 tsp olive oil
2 cups lamb stock; or 1 can (14 ½ oz) beef broth plus ¼ cup water, divided
¾ lb mushrooms; sliced
1 onion; chopped
2 garlic cloves; minced
1 lb red-skinned potatoes; cut into ¾ in. cubes
1 ½ tsp chopped fresh thyme; or dried thyme leaves, crushed
1 ½ tsp fresh rosemary; chopped, or dried rosemary, crushed
3 Tbsp fresh parsley; finely chopped
cobbler dough (see below)
1 egg yolk
1 Tbsp milk

Directions:

1. Preheat oven to 375 °F.
2. Season lamb to taste with salt and pepper; coat with flour.
3. Heat oil in Dutch oven over medium-high heat. Add lamb and brown on all sides. Remove lamb from pan and reserve.
4. Add ½ cup stock, mushrooms, onion, and garlic; cook until liquid has evaporated and onion is tender, stirring to scrape all brown bits from pan.
5. Add remaining 1 ½ cups stock, potatoes, thyme, and rosemary; cover and bring to a boil. Reduce heat to low; add lamb. Simmer, partially covered, 45 minutes or until lamb is tender. Season to taste with additional salt and pepper, if desired. Stir in chopped parsley.*
6. On a lightly floured surface, roll dough to ¼ in. thick. Using a cookie cutter, cut dough, reroll scraps, and cut more shapes.
7. Ladle lamb mixture into 1 ½ qt. casserole or 10-in. deep-dish pie plate. Top dough with cutouts, clustering and overlapping leaves lightly, allowing open spaces for steam to escape.
8. Beat together egg yolk and milk; brush dough with mixture. Bake 15 to 20 minutes or until top is golden brown.

To prepare cobbler dough:

1. Combine 1 cup flour, 1 Tbsp sugar, 1 tsp baking powder, and ½ tsp salt in small bowl.
2. Stir in ½ cup heavy cream; mix just until blended. Gather dough into ball.

* Sauce should be the consistency of gravy. If it's too thin, remove lamb and vegetables to casserole. Boil the sauce to reduce it to desired consistency.

Yield: 6 servings

ETHNIC

CONTENTS

LAMB ENCHILADAS WITH SALSA

¾ lb lean ground lamb
1 clove garlic; minced
½ cup green pepper; chopped
¼ cup celery; chopped
8 (6-in.) flour tortillas
½ cup green onions; diced
½ cup Mozzarella or Monterey Jack cheese (2 oz)
lite sour cream or plain yogurt
1 jar (16 oz) green or red salsa

Directions:

1. Preheat oven to 350 °F.
2. In a skillet, cook lamb, garlic, green pepper, and celery until no pink remains and vegetables are crisp and tender. Drain well.
3. Soften tortillas according to package instructions. Spoon meat mixture onto each tortilla, then roll up.
4. Place the filled tortillas, seam-side down, in an 11 × 7 baking dish. Top with salsa and cover with foil.
5. Bake at 350 °F for 20 minutes.
6. Uncover, sprinkle with cheese. Return to oven for 5 minutes to melt cheese. Garnish with sour cream and diced green onion.

Yield: 4 servings

LAMB CURRY

Lamb curry is an exotic way of using leftover lamb. It is usually served with a variety of condiments: chutney, watermelon pickles, grated coconut, ground peanuts, sliced candied ginger, sliced bananas, golden raisins and sliced onions.

2 cups cooked lamb; finely chopped
4 stalks celery
1 medium onion
1 medium apple; peeled
3 Tbsp butter or margarine
2 Tbsp all-purpose flour
1 Tbsp plus 1 tsp curry powder
1 tsp each Worcestershire sauce and seasoned salt
¼ tsp garlic salt
2 cups hot lamb broth; chicken or beef bouillon
coconut for garnish
1 cup rice; cooked according to package directions

Directions:

1. Trim fat from lamb. Finely chop by hand or use food processor with metal blade. Place lamb in bowl and set aside.
2. In same way, finely chop celery, onion and apple.
3. In large skillet, melt butter over medium heat. Sauté celery, onion and apple for 7 minutes. Add flour and seasonings blending thoroughly. Cook about 2 minutes, stirring constantly.
4. Add heated lamb broth and stir until mixture boils. Add lamb. Simmer, for 12 to 15 minutes. Thin with additional bouillon or milk if mixture becomes too thick.
5. Transfer to serving bowl. Sprinkle with coconut. Serve with cooked rice and condiments as listed above, if desired.

Yield: 4 servings

MOROCCAN-SPICED LAMB CHOPS

8 rib lamb chops
¾ tsp nutmeg; freshly grated
¼ tsp ground cloves
1 tsp black pepper; freshly ground
1 tsp white pepper; freshly ground
1 ½ tsp ground cinnamon
2 tsp ground cardamom
¼ tsp ground cayenne
pepper; to taste
¼ tsp ground cumin
¼ tsp ground turmeric
½ tsp sea salt
2 Tbsp olive or grapeseed oil

Directions:

1. In a shallow bowl, combine the nutmeg, cloves, black and white peppers, cinnamon, cardamom, cayenne, cumin, turmeric and salt.
2. Pat the lamb dry. Lightly sprinkle some of the spice blend over both sides of the lamb chops, saving the rest for another use. Rub spice blend evenly over lamb.
3. Place a large skillet over medium-high heat. Add the oil and heat until hot. Add the lamb, and cook, turning once, until done to your liking, about 5 minutes per side for medium-rare, depending on the thickness.
4. Transfer chops to a platter. Let rest for 5 minutes before serving.

Yield: 4 servings

COCONUT CURRY LAMB (SOUTH INDIAN)

1 lb lamb; trimmed of fat and cut into 1-in. pieces
¼ cup whole unsalted cashews
salt and freshly ground pepper; to taste
¼ cup vegetable oil
¼ tsp black mustard seeds
¼ tsp cumin seeds
¼ tsp ground coriander
1 Tbsp curry powder (see recipe see page 95)
1 medium onion; thinly sliced
1 tsp ginger root; finely grated
1 garlic clove; minced
1 can (14 oz) unsweetened coconut milk
¼ cup frozen peas
2 Tbsp chopped cilantro

Directions:

1. Preheat oven to 350 °F.
2. Spread the cashews in a pie plate and bake 5 minutes, or until fragrant and slightly toasted. Transfer to a plate to cool.
3. Lightly season the lamb with salt and pepper. In a large deep skillet, heat 3 Tbsp oil until smoking. Add the lamb and cook over medium-high heat 1 ½ minutes per side until golden brown. Transfer the lamb to a plate and reduce the heat to medium.
4. Add remaining 1 Tbsp oil to skillet and heat until smoking. Add mustard seeds and cook 1 minute, or until they stop popping. Add the cumin seeds, coriander, and curry powder and cook, stirring occasionally, about 1 minute, until fragrant. Add the onions, ginger, and garlic and cook 10 to 12 minutes until the onion softens. If mixture seems dry, add up to ¼ cup water to prevent sticking.
5. Stir in coconut milk and bring to a boil. Reduce heat to low. Return the lamb to skillet and simmer 5 to 8 minutes until cooked through. Stir in the peas and cook 1 minute. Transfer curry to a bowl, sprinkle with cilantro, and serve.

Yield: 4 servings

CURRY POWDER

2 Tbsp whole coriander seeds
1 Tbsp whole cumin seeds
2 tsp whole peppercorns
1 ½ tsp whole brown yellow mustard seeds
1 tsp whole fenugreek
5 whole cloves
3 dried hot red chile peppers; (crumbled)
1 ½ tsp ground turmeric

Directions:

1. Heat a small, heavy skillet over medium heat.
2. Add the coriander, cumin, peppercorns, mustard seeds, fenugreek seeds, cloves, and chiles.
3. Stir 5 minutes until the spices smell aromatic and toasted (a few spices will darken).
4. Add turmeric, stir 10 seconds.
5. Turn out onto a clean plate to cool.
6. Transfer spices to a coffee or spice grinder, in batches if necessary. Grind finely.
7. Use immediately or store in an air-tight container in a cool, dry place for up to 2 months.
8. This will only make 5 Tbsp, but it can be increased according to usage very easily.

RHODESIAN MEAT BALLS (KEFTEDES RODITIKI)

2 ½ lb ground lamb
⅔ cup dried whole wheat bread crumbs
2 ½ cups onions; coarsely chopped
1 ½ cups fresh flat leaf parsley; coarsely chopped
½ cup grated ripe tomato; or canned diced tomatoes with the juice
1 Tbsp aleppo pepper (or a pinch of crushed red pepper flakes or plenty of freshly ground black pepper)
1 Tbsp dried oregano; crumbled
1 tsp salt; or to taste
½ cup fresh mint leaves; packed
¼ cup ouzo, vodka, or water
1 cup all-purpose flour
olive oil and safflower oil for frying

Directions:

1. In a food processor, combine the bread crumbs, onions, parsley, tomato, pepper or pepper flakes, oregano, and salt.
2. Pulse to chop, scraping the sides of the bowl, just until the mixtures is uniform. Do not over-process.
3. Add the mint and pulse a few more times to chop.
4. In a large bowl, combine the meat, onion mixture, and ouzo, vodka, or water. Knead with your hands to mix. Cover and refrigerate for 1 to 3 hours.
5. Spread the flour on a large plate. Shape ¼ cup portions of the meat mixture into large meat balls. Flatten them slightly, dredge in the flour, and place on a sheet of aluminum foil.
6. In a large, deep skillet, heat 1 ½ in. of a combination of olive and safflower oil over medium-high heat to 350 °F. Add a few Keftedes at a time—do not crowd the skillet—and fry, turning them two or three times, until golden brown, about 4 minutes.
7. Transfer them to paper towels to drain. Serve hot, warm, or at room temperature.

Yield: about 30 meat balls to serve 6 to 8.

GERMAN LAMB IN SOUR CREAM

2 lb lean, boneless lamb; cut into chunks
1 large onion; chopped
1 ½ cups beef broth
2 Tbsp vegetable oil
1 tsp tarragon vinegar
½ cup flour; plus 2 Tbsp
2 tsp salt
2 Tbsp water
½ tsp dill seed
1 cup sour cream
½ tsp caraway seed
¼ tsp rosemary leaves

Directions:

1. Combine the first measure of flour with the salt, dill seed, caraway seed, and rosemary. Toss the lamb cubes in the mixture to coat thoroughly. Place the lamb cubes in a lightly oiled slow cooker.
2. Stir in all the remaining ingredients except the second measure of flour, the water, and the sour cream.
3. Cover. Cook on LOW for 10 to 14 hours. Turn to HIGH 30 minutes before serving.
4. Combine the second measure of flour with the water. Stir into the slow cooker.
5. Cover. Cook until thickened.
6. Stir in the sour cream.
7. Serve over hot buttered noodles and garnish with additional sour cream.

Yield: 4 servings

AFRICAN LAMB AND PEANUT STEW (WEIGHT WATCHERS)

1 ½ lb boned leg of lamb; trimmed and cut into 1-in. cubes
cooking spray
2 tsp peanut oil
4 cups onion; thinly sliced
8 garlic cloves; minced
1 Tbsp ground coriander
1 Tbsp ground cumin
1 tsp ground red pepper
4 cups water
1 large peeled sweet potato; cut into 1-in. pieces
2 large carrots; cut into 1-in. pieces
⅓ cup reduced-fat chunky peanut butter
¼ cup tomato paste
2 (14 ½ oz) cans diced tomatoes; drained
1 tsp salt
1 tsp freshly ground black pepper
2 cups sliced fresh or frozen cut okra
4 cups hot cooked long-grain rice

Directions:

1. Heat a large Dutch oven over medium-high heat. Coat lamb with cooking spray.
2. Add lamb to pan; cook 5 minutes or until brown, stirring frequently. Drain in a colander; set aside. Wipe drippings from pan with a paper towel.
3. Recoat Dutch oven with cooking spray; add oil. Place over medium-high heat.
4. Add onion and garlic; cook 2 minutes, stirring constantly. Return lamb to pan, and add coriander, cumin, and red pepper. Cook 2 minutes, stirring constantly.
5. Add water and next 7 ingredients; stir well, and bring to a boil. Cover, reduce heat, and simmer 30 minutes. Add okra, and cook an additional 5 minutes.
6. Spoon rice into individual bowls; top with stew.

Yield: 7 servings (2 cups stew and about ½ cup rice each)

SPANISH LAMB WITH RICE (ARROZ CON CORDERO)

2 lb lamb leg; trimmed of any fat and cut into 1-in. or bite-sized serving pieces
1 Tbsp olive oil
1 large onion; chopped
1 large red bell pepper; cut into ½-in. pieces
4 garlic cloves; minced
2 tsp paprika
2 cups long-grain white rice
1 ¼ cups red wine
1 can (15 oz) diced tomatoes; including the juice
1 ¾ cups stock; (vegetable, chicken, veal, or lamb)
⅛ tsp saffron thread; crumbled
1 bay leaf
1 cup frozen peas; (not thawed)
½ cup pimiento-stuffed green olives; coarsely chopped
fresh flat-leaf parsley; chopped

Directions:

1. Season the meat with salt and pepper.
2. Heat oil in a 12-in. heavy skillet (2 in. deep or more) over medium-high heat until hot but not smoking.
3. Brown the lamb on all sides until browned and no longer pink.
4. Transfer the meat to a plate with tongs and set aside.
5. Pour off all but 2 Tbsp of fat from the skillet.
6. Add the onion and bell pepper.
7. Cook over medium heat, stirring, until softened (about 5 to 8 minutes).
8. Add the garlic, paprika, and rice.
9. Cook, stirring 1 to 2 minutes.
10. Add the wine and boil, uncovered (about 2 minutes).
11. Stir in the tomatoes with the juice, broth or stock, saffron, and bay leaf.
12. Add the meat back into the rice mixture, adding any juices that are on the plate.
13. Cook, covered, over low heat until the meat is heated and cooked through, the rice is tender, and most of the liquid has been absorbed (about another 15 minutes).
14. Remove from the heat and stir in the peas and olives. Cover and let stand for 10 minutes.
15. Discard the bay leaf.

Yield: 4 servings.

INDIAN LAMB ROGAN JOSH (PRESSURE COOKER)

This is a classic Indian curry that's perfect for a party. Use lean lamb and marinate overnight for layers of deep, rich flavor.

2 lb lean lamb shoulder; trimmed and cut into chunks
½ cup plain yogurt
4 green cardamom pods
1 small cinnamon stick or ½ tsp ground cinnamon
2 tsp paprika
1 tsp turmeric
1 tsp ground coriander
1 tsp ground cumin
½ tsp cayenne pepper
2 tsp garam masala
2 cups canned tomatoes
2 cloves garlic; peeled
1 large onion; chopped
1 piece (2-in.) ginger root
3 Tbsp vegetable oil
1 cup water
2 Tbsp chopped cilantro sprigs for garnish

Directions:

1. In a bowl or resealable plastic bag, toss lamb with yogurt.
2. In a blender or spice grinder, pulverize whole cardamom and cinnamon. Add to lamb mixture with paprika, turmeric, coriander, cumin, and cayenne. Cover and refrigerate overnight.
3. In a food processor, combine garam masala, tomatoes, garlic, onions, and ginger; purée until smooth.
4. In a pressure cooker, heat oil over medium heat. Add tomato mixture and cook for 5 minutes. Stir in lamb and marinade. Stir in water. Lock the lid in place and bring cooker up to full pressure over medium-high heat. Reduce heat to medium-low, just to maintain even pressure, and cook for 20 minutes. Remove from heat and release pressure quickly. The lamb should be fork tender. If not, return to full pressure and cook for another 5 minutes. Release pressure quickly.
5. Remove lid and bring to boil. Reduce heat and simmer curry until nicely thickened.
6. Stir in cilantro just before serving. Garnish with cilantro sprigs.

Yield: 4 to 6 servings

TAMED LAMB VINDALOO WITH SPINACH AND POTATOES (PRESSURE COOKER)

2 lb boneless lamb shoulder or leg; cut into 1 in. cubes
1 to 2 Tbsp vegetable oil
1 large onion; peeled, halved, and thinly sliced
2 tsp whole cumin seeds
¼ cup water
1 can (14 oz) unsweetened coconut milk
2 Tbsp Dijon mustard
1 tsp salt; or to taste
1 tsp turmeric
¼ tsp cayenne pepper; or more to taste
2 packages (10 oz) frozen chopped spinach
1 ½ lb Yukon Gold potatoes; peeled and cut into 2 in. chunks (no smaller)

Directions:

1. Over medium-high heat, heat 1 Tbsp oil in the pressure cooker. Cook the onion, stirring frequently, for 2 minutes.
2. Add the lamb, cumin seeds, and more oil if needed, and cook until the lamb loses its pink color, stirring frequently 2 to 3 minutes.
3. Add the water and stir well, taking care to scrape up any browned bits stuck to the bottom of the cooker.
4. Add the coconut milk and blend in the mustard, salt, turmeric, and cayenne.
5. Add the frozen blocks of spinach and set the potatoes on top.
6. Lock the cooker's lid in place. Over high heat, bring to high pressure. Lower the heat to maintain high pressure and cook for 20 minutes. Quick-release the pressure. Remove the lid, tilting it away from you to allow any excess steam to escape.
7. If you wish, slash the potatoes into bite-sized pieces. Stir the vindaloo well, and add more cayenne, mustard, and salt, if needed.

Note: To "untame" this recipe, add chili flakes, to taste.

Yield: 4 servings

⟁ SAMOOSAS (SAMBOUSA, ARABIC EGGROLL)

1 lb ground lamb
½ carrot; minced
½ onion; minced
1 clove garlic; minced
1 tsp tomato paste
1 green onion; chopped
1 pinch seasoning salt
1 green chile pepper; diced (optional)
1 package (16 oz) egg roll wrappers; cut in half into rectangles
1 Tbsp all-purpose flour
1 Tbsp water
2 cups vegetable oil

Directions:

1. In a large skillet, brown meat. Remove the meat from the skillet.
2. In the same skillet used for the meat, sauté onion, garlic, carrot, and green onion. When the vegetables are tender, add tomato paste and seasoning salt. Stir in browned meat.
3. In a small bowl, combine flour with water until a watery paste is formed. Place 1 tsp meat mixture in the front part of one of the strips. Starting from the right front corner, fold over to the left. You've started the triangle shape. Continue back and forth (making a triangular shape) until there is no more wrapper. Seal the wrappers closed with the flour and water mixture. Continue this process until all of the ingredients are used.
4. Using oil to taste, fry the triangular packages until crisp.

SOUPS AND STEWS

CONTENTS

SOUTHERN STYLE LAMB HASH

2 lb to 3 lb lamb shoulder; trimmed of all excess fat and cut into chunks
1 cup onions; coarsely chopped
2 Tbsp bacon grease or olive oil
1 whole chicken; cut up
1 bay leaf
2 Tbsp cracked pepper
1 can (28 oz) canned tomatoes
1 cup cider vinegar; more or less to your taste
2 tsp salt
1 tsp Tabasco
1 Tbsp molasses or brown sugar

Directions:

1. In a large Dutch pot, sauté the onions in the fat or oil over medium-high heat until just golden.
2. Brown the lamb.
3. Add water to barely cover.
4. Add the bay leaf and pepper.
5. Raise the heat. Bring to a boil. Cover.
6. Reduce the heat to a simmer. Cook at least 1 hour, until the chicken is falling from the bones.
7. Use a slotted spoon to pull the chicken and the lamb from the stew. Place in a colander.
8. When cool enough to handle, pull all the meat from the bones and chop into small pieces. Discard the skin, bones, and fat.
9. Return the meat to the Dutch pot and the cooking liquid.
10. Mash the tomatoes in their juice and add to the Dutch pot along with the vinegar, salt, Tabasco, and molasses.
11. Add any other flavors you normally like in a barbecue sauce, e.g., mustard, ketchup, Worcestershire, etc.
12. Add veggies such as potatoes, corn, carrots, green beans.
13. Simmer the mixture uncovered until it is the consistency that you prefer... about 1 hour to be like a stew...longer to cook down to a pudding style.

Yield: about 12 generous servings

KENTUCKY BURGOO

What is burgoo? One possible origin of the word "burgoo" is "burghul," an Ara-bic word for crushed grain. This theory derives from a 17th century version of burgoo, which was a porridge served to sailors. Burgoo, also called "Kentucky Burgoo," now refers to a stew slow-cooked in large kettles. The Kentucky con-nection comes from two colorful characters of the 1930s, renowned burgoo-maker J.T. Looney and his Kentucky Derby-winning horse, Burgoo King.

2 lb boneless lamb shoulder; trimmed of excess fat
2 Tbsp vegetable oil
2 lb boneless beef shank; trimmed of excess fat
salt and freshly ground black pepper; to taste
2 medium onions; quartered
4 cloves garlic; peeled
1 medium fresh hot red pepper; quartered
1 (3-lb to 4-lb) whole chicken or hen; cut into 8 pieces
2 cups onions; chopped
2 cups carrots; medium-diced
1 cup green bell peppers; medium-diced
1 lb baking potatoes; such as russets, peeled and medium-diced
2 cups tomatoes; peeled, seeded and chopped
½ lb fresh green beans; strings removed and cut into 2-in. pieces
2 cups fresh corn kernels
2 Tbsp light-brown sugar
1 Tbsp fresh parsley leaves; finely chopped

Directions:

1. Heat oil in a large, heavy pot over medium heat.
2. Season the lamb and beef with salt and pepper. When the oil is hot, sear the meat, in batches, for a couple of minutes on all sides. Add the onion quarters, garlic, and hot red pepper.
3. Cover with water (it may take about 3 to 4 quarts). Bring to a boil, reduce the heat to medium-low, and simmer for 1 ½ hours.
4. Season chicken with salt and pepper. Add to pot; cook 1 ½ hours longer.
5. When meat and chicken are tender, remove them from the pot, set aside, and let cool. Remove cooked vegetables from pot; discard.
6. To the pot of hot liquid, add chopped onions, carrots, bell pepper, potatoes, tomatoes, green beans, corn, and brown sugar. Cook for 1 hour.
7. After the meat has cooled, cube the beef and lamb into 1-in. pieces. Remove the skin and bones from the chicken and discard. Dice the chicken into 1-in. pieces.
8. Add the cubed meat and chicken to the vegetables; cook for 30 minutes longer. Reseason if necessary.
9. Ladle the stew into serving bowls. Serve with hot corn bread or biscuits. Garnish with parsley.

Yield: 16 servings

MEDITERRANEAN LAMB AND SQUASH STEW

1 lb boneless lamb shoulder
½ tsp pepper
2 tsp oil
1 onion; chopped
1 clove garlic; mashed
½ tsp paprika
1 ½ cups beef stock
1 ½ tsp dried mint
1 tsp lemon rind; grated
2 cups butternut or buttercup squash; peeled and cubed
½ lb green beans; trimmed
1 Tbsp red wine vinegar

Directions:

1. Trim fat from lamb; cut into bite-size pieces. Sprinkle with pepper.
2. In Dutch oven, heat oil over medium-high heat; brown lamb, in batches, for 5 minutes; transfer to plate.
3. Reduce heat to medium; cook onion, garlic and paprika for about 4 minutes or until softened.
4. Add stock, mint and lemon rind; bring to boil, scraping up brown bits.
5. Add lamb, reduce heat, cover, and simmer for 1 hour.
6. Stir in squash; cover and simmer for 15 minutes or until lamb is tender.
7. Meanwhile, cut beans into 1-in. pieces, add to stew and simmer for 12 to 15 minutes or until tender-crisp.
8. Stir in vinegar.

Yield: 4 servings

GREEK LAMB AND BEAN STEW

1 lb lean boneless lamb; cut in 1-in. pieces
2 cups dried large lima beans
2 Tbsp oil
1 Spanish onion; chopped
4 cloves garlic; minced
1 Tbsp dried oregano
½ Tbsp hot pepper flakes
1 can (19 oz) tomatoes; chopped
1 tsp salt
½ tsp pepper
1 each large red and green pepper; chopped
½ cup Kalamata olives; rinsed
¼ cup fresh parsley; chopped

Directions:

1. Sort and rinse beans. In large saucepan, bring beans and 8 cups cold water to boil; cover and cook for 15 minutes. Drain and return to pot.
2. Add 8 cups water; bring to boil. Reduce heat and simmer; partially covered, for 45 minutes or until tender. Drain.
3. Meanwhile, in large Dutch oven, heat half of the oil over high heat; brown lamb, in batches if necessary. Transfer to plate.
4. Add remaining oil to pan; reduce heat to medium. Add onion, garlic, oregano and hot pepper flakes; cook, stirring, for 5 minutes or until softened.
5. Return meat to pan along with any juices. Add tomatoes, salt and pepper; bring to boil. Reduce heat, cover and simmer for 45 minutes.
6. Add beans, red and green peppers, olives and enough water to make it a sauce-like consistency.
7. Bake, covered, in 350 °F oven for about 40 minutes or until lamb is tender. (Stew can be cooled in refrigerator and stored in airtight container for up to 3 days or frozen for up to 1 month).
8. Stir in parsley.

Yield: 4 servings

OVEN LAMB STEW

2 Tbsp vegetable oil
2 lb lean lamb; cut into 1-in. cubes
1 medium onion; sliced
2 cups water
1 Tbsp Worcestershire sauce
2 Tbsp unbleached all-purpose flour
3 Tbsp cold water
1 cup peas; fresh or frozen
3 medium carrots; sliced
1 stalk of celery; sliced
salt and freshly ground black pepper; to taste

Directions:

1. Preheat oven to 325 °F.
2. In a large heavy skillet, heat the oil and brown the lamb.
3. Add the onion and sauté for 5 minutes, stirring frequently.
4. Drain off the fat. Add the water and Worcestershire.
5. Bake, covered, for 1 ½ hours.
6. Remove the skillet from the oven.
7. In a small bowl, blend the flour with the water to make a thin paste.
8. Add the paste to the skillet and blend well.
9. Add the peas, carrots, celery, and salt and pepper to taste. Bake, covered, for 30 minutes longer.
10. Serve.

Yield: 1 ½ quarts

NO PEEK STEW

2 lb lean lamb stew meat; cut into small pieces
1 can cream of mushroom soup
1 package dry onion soup mix
1 cup water

Directions:

1. Mix all ingredients in a 2-quart casserole with a tight fitting lid.
2. Bake at 300 °F for 3 hours. NO PEEKING!
3. Serve with buttered noodles or cooked rice sprinkled with poppy seeds.

MASTER LAMB STEW

1 lb leg of lamb; cut into 1-in. cubes
3 lb lamb neck bones with meat
¼ cup oil; divided
2 cups onions; minced
3 cloves garlic; crushed and coarsely chopped
3 Tbsp sweet Hungarian paprika
1 bay leaf
1 sprig of thyme
1 tsp salt; or to taste
3 tomatoes; peeled, seeded and chopped
2 cups steamed root vegetables; a mixture of rutabaga, turnip, parsnip cut into ½- in.
    cubes
2 cups cooked flat buttered noodles
cracked black pepper; to taste
fresh thyme leaves for garnish

Directions:

1. Place bones in a non-reactive Dutch pot. Add enough cold water to cover. Bring to a boil.
2. Reduce heat to medium-low and simmer for 5 minutes. Drain and rinse bones under cold water. Set aside.
3. Rinse pot to remove any sediment. Set the Dutch pot over medium-high heat. Add 3 Tbsp oil.
4. Add onions and garlic and cook 2 to 3 minutes until onions begin to brown.
5. Reduce heat to low and continue cooking for 10 minutes until the onions are golden. Stir occasionally to keep the onions from burning.
6. Remove Dutch pot from the heat and stir in paprika.
7. Add rinsed bones and 6 cups water. Add bay leaf, thyme sprig, and 1 tsp of salt. Bring to a boil. Reduce heat and simmer, partially covered for 1 hour.
8. Skim broth to remove any foam while cooking.
9. Remove bones, bay leaf, and thyme from broth and skim any fat or foam.
10. Broth can be refrigerated at this point for up to 3 days. If the broth has been refrigerated, heat it to a simmer and proceed.
11. Add tomatoes and bring to a boil.
12. Reduce heat to a simmer and cook, partially covered for 15 minutes until slightly thickened.
13. Add salt to taste.
14. In a heavy skillet, brown the meat in the remaining 1 Tbsp of oil over medium-high heat for 2 to 3 minutes until the meat is medium-rare.
15. Spoon broth into 4 large bowls. Spoon meat into the center of each bowl and surround it with steamed vegetables. Spoon noodles on the side. Sprinkle with cracked black pepper and fresh thyme.

Yield: 4 servings...but can be multiplied to feed a crowd.

IRISH STEW (CROCK POT)

2 lb lean lamb stew meat
6 medium potatoes (2 lb); cut into ½ in. slices
3 medium onions; sliced
1 tsp salt
¼ tsp pepper
1 tsp dried thyme leaves
1 can (14 ½ oz) ready-to-serve beef broth
fresh parsley; chopped (optional)

Directions:

1. Layer ½ each of lamb, potatoes, and onions in a 3 ½ to 6 quart slow cooker.
2. Sprinkle with ½ each of salt, pepper, and thyme.
3. Repeat layers and sprinkle with remaining seasonings. Pour broth over top.
4. Cover and cook on low for 8 to 10 hours (or high 3 to 5 hours) or until lamb and vegetables are tender.
5. Skim fat from stew. Sprinkle parsley over stew.

Yield: 8 servings

SUPER SUPER BOWL JAMBALAYA

1 lb ground lamb (shoulder); browned and drained of any excess fat
6 Tbsp olive oil
1 large green bell pepper; seeded and chopped
1 large red bell pepper; seeded and chopped
2 Tbsp tomato paste
1 cup raw long-grained rice
1 container (32 oz) chicken broth; low-sodium, low-fat
1 box (8-oz) Zatarain's New Orleans Style Jambalaya mix
1 tsp freshly ground black pepper
1 tsp cayenne pepper
2 cans (8-oz) tomato sauce
1 lb medium shrimp; shelled and deveined
water; as needed

Directions:

1. In a large Dutch pot (or other nonreactive pot) heat the oil over medium-high heat.
2. Add the lamb and bell peppers, sauté for 3 minutes.
3. Add the tomato paste, raw long-grained rice, and 1 cup chicken broth. Mix to combine and cook 1 minute.
4. Add remaining broth and stir. Bring to a boil.
5. Add Jambalaya mix, black pepper, cayenne, tomato sauce, and shrimp. Cover. Reduce heat and simmer 25 minutes, stirring occasionally or until the rice is tender. If mixture becomes too dry while simmering, add a little bit of water.

LAMB STEW WITH ENDIVE AND CARROT

2 Tbsp butter or olive oil
1 ½ lb lamb shoulder or breast; trimmed of excess fat and diced into ¾-in. pieces
4 heads Belgian endive
4 medium carrots; peeled and cut into 2-in. lengths
salt and freshly ground black pepper; to taste
1 cup chicken, beef, or vegetable stock or broth
2 Tbsp Dijon mustard; optional
2 Tbsp fresh or sour cream; optional
parsley; chopped, for garnish

Directions:

1. Put butter or oil in a large nonreactive skillet and turn the heat to high. When the butter melts or the oil is hot, add the meat in one layer. Cook about 5 minutes, or until the lamb is just browned on one side. Stir once, then move the lamb to one side of the pan.
2. With the heat on high, add whole endives in one layer and scatter the carrots all over. Cook 1 to 2 minutes until the endives brown on one side. Turn and cook another minute, then sprinkle all with salt and pepper.
3. Add stock or broth. Stir. Let cook for 1 minute. Then turn heat to very low and cover. Cook about 30 minutes or so until tender, stirring once. If necessary, turn heat to high until the sauce thickens a bit. Taste and adjust the seasonings.
4. *Sauce*: Remove meat and veggies to platter. Blend mustard and cream and stir into sauce in pan until smooth. Pour over meat and vegetables. Garnish with parsley and serve.

Yield: 4 servings

MISCELLANEOUS

CONTENTS

DELI-STYLE CORNED LAMB

4 lb to 6 lb lamb; (any solid cut)
5 Tbsp Morton Tender Quick
2 tsp brown sugar
1 Tbsp ground black pepper
1 tsp ground paprika
1 tsp ground bay leaves
1 tsp ground allspice
½ tsp garlic powder

Directions:

1. Trim surface tallow from brisket.
2. In small box, mix Morton Tender Quick and remaining ingredients.
3. Rub mixture into all sides of brisket. Place brisket in a resealable plastic bag. Refrigerate and allow to cure 5 days per inch of meat thickness.
4. Place cured brisket in Dutch oven. Add water to cover. Bring to a boil; reduce heat. Simmer until tender, about 3 to 4 hours.

Yield: 5 to 8 servings

⚐ LAMB DIJON (CROCK POT)

2 lb lamb stew meat
¼ cup all-purpose flour
1 tsp salt
¼ tsp pepper
2 Tbsp vegetable oil
6 new potatoes (1 ¼ lb); cubed
¼ cup Dijon mustard
½ tsp grated lemon peel
1 Tbsp lemon juice
2 tsp rosemary leaves; chopped fresh or ½ tsp dried
2 cloves garlic; finely chopped
1 can (14 ½ oz) ready-to-serve beef broth
package (10 oz) frozen green peas; thawed

Directions:

1. Mix flour, salt, and pepper in a resealable plastic bag. Add lamb; shake until evenly coated.
2. Heat oil in 12-in. skillet over medium-high heat. Cook lamb in oil about 20 minutes, stirring occasionally, until brown; drain on towels.
3. Mix lamb and remaining ingredients except peas in 3 ½- to 6-quart slow cooker. Cover and cook on low heat setting 8 to 10 hours, until lamb is tender.
4. Skim fat from the juices in cooker. Stir peas into lamb mixture.
5. Cover and cook on high heat setting 10 to 15 minutes, until peas are hot.

Yield: 6 servings

◺ EGGPLANT AND ROASTED LAMB "SANDWICHES"

½ lb roasted leg of lamb; thinly sliced (rare as possible)
1 large, firm eggplant
salt and freshly ground pepper; to taste
olive oil
2 eggs
2 Tbsp water
1 cup fine dry bread crumbs
1 tsp fresh thyme; finely chopped
basil sabayon; (recipe follows)
fried basil leaves; for garnish (optional)

Directions:

1. Preheat oven to 425 °F.
2. Cut eight round ¼-in.-thick slices from the eggplant, discarding the ends. Season them generously with salt and pepper. Brush them all over liberally with olive oil. Place four of the slices on a baking sheet and top them with slices of the lamb, dividing the meat evenly. Do not let the meat protrude from the edge. Top with the remaining eggplant slices.
3. In a flat bowl, beat the eggs with the water. In another bowl or plate, place the bread crumbs, mixed with thyme. Dip the sandwiches one at a time into the egg to moisten them, then roll them in the bread crumbs. Shake off the excess and return them to the baking sheet.
4. Bake the eggplant sandwiches for 10 to 15 minutes on each side, or until they are crisp and brown. Serve on a heated plate with Basil Sabayon drizzled around it. Top with a fried basil leaf (optional).

Yield: Serves 4

Basil Sabayon

¼ cup shredded basil leaves
¼ cup dry white wine
6 egg yolks
4 tsp vinegar
Salt; to taste

1. Boil the basil and white wine in a non-aluminum saucepan until the liquid reduces to less than 1 Tbsp.
2. Blend in the egg yolks and cook over very low heat (a double boiler is preferable), whisking constantly until the mixture becomes airy and thick.
3. Stir in the vinegar and salt. Keep sauce warm but do not let it come close to boiling, or it will curdle.

SPINACH SALAD WITH LAMB AND BASIL

1 ½ lb boneless lamb loin
½ cup plus 2 Tbsp extra-virgin olive oil
3 Tbsp fresh basil leaves; finely chopped
3 red bell peppers; roasted and peeled
2 Tbsp aged red-wine vinegar
10 oz soft mild goat cheese
1 bunch spinach; (about 6 cups packed)

Directions:

1. Trim and tie lamb. Season lamb with salt and pepper and in a resealable plastic bag combine lamb, 2 Tbsp oil, and 1 Tbsp basil, turning lamb to coat evenly. Marinate lamb, covered and chilled, 4 hours.
2. Preheat oven to 450 °F.
3. Cut roasted peppers into thin 2-in.-long strips and in a bowl combine with vinegar and 2 Tbsp oil. Chill peppers, covered, until assembling salad.
4. In another bowl, coarsely crumble goat cheese and gently stir together with 2 Tbsp oil and 1 Tbsp basil. Chill goat cheese, covered, until assembling salad.
5. In a blender, blend remaining ¼ cup oil, remaining Tbsp basil, and salt and pepper to taste until smooth. Transfer basil oil to a small bowl.
6. Chill basil oil, covered, while preparing lamb. Bring basil oil to room temperature before assembling salad.
7. Heat an ovenproof heavy skillet (preferably cast-iron) over medium-high heat until hot, and brown lamb on all sides. Put skillet in middle of oven and roast lamb about 10 minutes, or until a meat thermometer registers 140 °F for medium-rare.
8. Cool lamb. Chill lamb, covered, at least 2 hours and up to 1 day. Cut lamb into thin slices.
9. Discard coarse stems from spinach and arrange leaves around edges of 4 large plates. Scatter some peppers evenly over spinach and mound some goat cheese in center of each plate. Arrange lamb slices around goat cheese and drizzle salads with basil oil.

Yield: 4 servings

LAMB-VEGETABLE RAGOUT

This is a tasty topper for pasta or rice. With the growing acceptance and trend toward "one-dish meals," this one surely fits the bill. Casual, quick, and convenient. Don't confuse the Sugar snap peas with snow peas; each kind has a different flavor and texture.

12 oz. (¾ lb) leg of lamb steak or loin; trimmed of visible fat and cut into ¾-in. pieces
1 Tbsp olive or vegetable oil
1 ½ cups sliced fresh shitake or button mushrooms (4 oz)
½ cup onions; chopped
2 cloves of garlic; minced
3 Tbsp flour
½ tsp salt; to taste
¼ tsp freshly ground pepper
1 can (15 oz) beef broth
¼ cup red wine or dry sherry
2 cups sugar snap peas or 1 package (10 oz) of the frozen sugar snap peas; thawed
1 cup cherry tomatoes; halved

Directions:

1. In a large nonstick skillet, heat the oil over medium-high heat.
2. Cool and stir the lamb in hot oil 3 to 5 minutes or until the lamb is to desired doneness. Remove the lamb and set aside.
3. In the same skillet, cook the mushrooms, onion, and garlic until tender.
4. Stir in the flour, salt, and pepper. Add the broth and wine. Cook and stir until thickened and bubbly.
5. Stir in the sugar snap peas. Cook and stir 3 to 4 minutes more or until the peas are tender.
6. Stir in the lamb and tomatoes. Heat through.

Note: Serve the lamb and vegetable mixture over hot bow-tie pasta or wide noodles. Serve with some crusty type of quality bread, and a tropical flavored sorbet for dessert.

Yield: 4 servings.

LAMB WITH CILANTRO

1 lb lean lamb; cut into thin strips
1 Tbsp cornstarch
1 tsp sugar
1 tsp sesame oil
2 Tbsp peanut oil
1 ¾ cups broccoli flowerets; sliced
3 dried black winter mushrooms; soaked in hot water 25 minutes, drained
2 green onions; chopped
1 garlic clove; finely chopped
2 tsp rice wine or dry sherry
1 Tbsp dark soy sauce
1 Tbsp fresh cilantro; finely chopped

Directions:

1. Place lamb in a dish. In a bowl, mix together cornstarch, sugar, and sesame oil and stir into lamb until well coated. Let stand 30 minutes.
2. In a wok, heat peanut oil, add lamb, and stir-fry 2 minutes. Remove lamb from wok and keep warm.
3. Add broccoli, mushrooms, green onions, and garlic and stir-fry about 5 minutes until broccoli is just tender.
4. Stir in rice wine or dry sherry, soy sauce, lamb, and cilantro. Stir over very high heat 1 minute.

Yield: 4 servings

LAMB AND PEPPER STIR-FRY (WEIGHT WATCHERS)

15 oz boneless lamb (from the loin); cut into thin strips
1 Tbsp plus 1 tsp vegetable oil
1 Tbsp plus 1 ½ tsp soy sauce
2 tsp honey
1 medium red bell pepper; cored, seeded and cut into ½ in. strips
1 medium yellow bell pepper; cored, seeded and cut into ½ in. strips
8 medium scallions; cut into 2-in. pieces
2 tsp garlic; finely chopped
2 tsp fresh ginger root; finely chopped
zest from 1 orange; julienned
¼ tsp crushed red pepper flakes; or to taste
2 Tbsp low-sodium chicken broth
coarsely ground black pepper; to taste
1 Tbsp fresh mint; chopped, to garnish (optional)

Directions:

1. Heat a nonstick wok or large skillet over high heat.
2. Add oil, then lamb, and stir-fry until lamb loses its red color, about 1 to 2 minutes. Remove with slotted spoon and reserve.
3. In measuring cup, combine soy sauce and honey; reserve.
4. Add bell peppers to wok; stir-fry until peppers soften slightly, about 4 minutes.
5. Add scallions, garlic, ginger, zest, red pepper flakes, and soy sauce mixture. Stir-fry 30 seconds more.
6. Return lamb to wok. Add broth and black pepper; stir-fry another 30 seconds to reheat lamb and blend flavors.
7. To serve, sprinkle mint over stir-fry, if desired.

Yield: 4 servings

WINNING LAMB MUFFALETTA

1 ½ lb pre-roasted lamb; thinly sliced
2 cups shredded lettuce
½ red onion; sliced
1 ½ cups green olives; stuffed or unstuffed
½ lb sliced mozzarella
1 loaf (6-in. or 14-in.) ciabatta bread
1 Tbsp oregano leaves
¼ cup extra-virgin olive oil
hot sauce; to taste

Directions:

1. Cut the loaf in half horizontally.
2. On the bottom half of loaf, layer the sliced lamb and cheese. Top with chopped olives, red onions, and shredded lettuce.
3. Combine the oil and oregano and sprinkle over the top half of the loaf. Sprinkle with hot sauce. Replace the top half of loaf over the fillings. Cut into small pieces.

MARINADES/RUBS

CONTENTS

BASIC BARBECUE RUB

¼ cup brown sugar; firmly packed
¼ cup sweet paprika
3 Tbsp black pepper
3 Tbsp coarse salt
1 Tbsp hickory smoked salt or coarse salt
2 tsp celery seeds
2 tsp garlic powder
2 tsp onion powder
1 tsp cayenne pepper

Directions:

1. Combine all the above ingredients in a mixing bowl and stir.
2. Store this rub in an airtight jar away from the heat. It will keep for about 6 months.

Yield: about 1 cup

BEER MARINADE FOR LAMB

2 cans beer
2 tsp salt
½ cup olive oil
1 tsp cayenne pepper
1 Tbsp wine vinegar
1 Tbsp prepared horseradish
1 tsp onion powder
2 Tbsp lemon juice
1 tsp garlic powder

Directions:

Mix all ingredients together and use as a marinade. Also use as a mop sauce during slow cooking.

SOUTHWEST MARINADE AND DRY RUB

Southwest Marinade Ingredients:
¼ cup pineapple juice
¼ cup orange juice
⅛ cup lime juice
⅛ cup soy sauce
⅛ cup liquid smoke

Dry Rub Ingredients:
⅛ tsp cayenne
¼ tsp paprika
¼ tsp garlic powder
⅛ tsp cumin
⅛ tsp chili powder
⅛ tsp sugar

Directions:

1. For a smoky, sassy, hot and sweet taste sensation, marinate meat in this concoction for about an hour.
2. Then rub meat in the dry rub mixture. Grill or broil.

LAMB AND GAME MARINADE

A marinade sauce to enhance the flavor of lamb, game, and other meat!

WARNING*** Any marinade coming in contact with raw meat, seafood, or poultry must be boiled for one minute before using it for basting.

¾ cup Cabernet Sauvignon or other dry red wine
¼ cup Balsamic vinegar
3 Tbsp olive oil
2 Tbsp unsulfured (light) molasses
2 Tbsp fresh thyme; chopped or 2 tsp dried
2 Tbsp fresh rosemary; chopped or 2 tsp dried
1 Tbsp crushed juniper berries or 2 Tbsp gin
3 large garlic cloves; minced
3 2-in. × 1-in. strips orange peel; (orange part only)
3 2-in. × 1-in. strips lemon peel; (yellow part only)
8 whole cloves
8 whole black peppercorns
2 bay leaves; broken in half
¾ tsp salt

Directions:

1. Mix all ingredients in medium bowl. (Can be made 2 days ahead. Cover and chill.) Marinate poultry 2 to 4 hours and meat 6 to 12 hours in refrigerator. Drain marinade into saucepan.
2. Boil 1 minute. Pat meat or poultry dry. Grill, basting occasionally with marinade.

Yield: about 1 ½ cups

INDEX

INDEX

A

B

C

D

E

F

G

H

I

J

⚞K

⚞L

R

S

T

⟋V

⟋W

⟋Y

⟋Z

⟋NUMERICS

Copies of this cookbook can be purchased from the BBSAI Web site at

www.blackbellysheep.org

Made in the USA
Lexington, KY
10 December 2012